The Ultimate Enlightenment For 2012
All We Need Is Ourselves

Michele Doucette

The Ultimate Enlightenment For 2012: All We Need Is Ourselves

Copyright © 2010 by Michele Doucette, St. Clair Publications

All rights reserved. No part of this publication may be reproduced or transmitted in any form or by any means, electronic or mechanical, including photocopying, recording, or by any information storage and retrieval system, without written permission from the author.

ISBN 978-0-9801704-0-5

Printed in the United States of America by

St. Clair Publications

PO Box 726

McMinnville, TN 37111-0726

http://stan.stclair.net

The key is to be in a state of permanent connectedness with your inner body – to feel it at all times. This will rapidly deepen and transform your life. The more consciousness you direct into the inner body, the higher its vibrational frequency becomes.

Eckhart Tolle

Table of Contents

Dedication 1
Personal Message 3
Author's Note 5
Reviews 8
Prologue 25
Introduction 26
Inner Rumblings 30
The Power of Thought 36
Prayers Are Always Answered 53
Spiritual Literacy aka The Spiritual Truth 62
Religious Affiliation Does Not Matter 77
Paradigm Shift 91
Transformation 96
Unplugging From The Matrix 103
Utopia Exists 112
Time To Wake Up 120
We Are Our Own Future 124
Quotable "The Secret" Quotes 130
We've Been Living In A Dream World 133

Peace Really Does Depend On You 141
She Created Me 148
Epilogue 156
Bibliography 164
About the Author 177

Dedication

For my dear friend Raita Kaarina Outinen Knuutila who transitioned on March 19, 2010, on the cusp of the spring equinox, a time of growth and renewal.

While she shall be dearly missed, I am at ease knowing that she is now experiencing, firsthand, the rejuvenating light and energy of the Creator.

While I knew her naught as a journalist and political writer, this was a woman who endured much, having lived in Karelia, Sweden, California, Japan, Equador, Greece, France, Egypt and, lastly, Finland.

When I released my first edition copy of *A Travel in Time to Grand Pré*, she was there to celebrate, right along with me, complete with music from Van Morrison, incense burning and dancing in the moonlight.

Life is but a journey to one's self. We are here to discover that we need not seek anything outside of our own Being. Some might prefer to call this a rediscovery of the true self.

The Ultimate Enlightenment For 2012

Be not afraid of change, I would often say to Raita, *because it is change that allows all to Be* (as they are) *and to Become* (who they truly are).

The ability to express forgiveness, allowing others the outcome of their own experience(s), without changing the nature of who you truly are, is the mastery to which all can attain. Therein lies the healing of all illusion, all separation, all duality.

Raita, a name that is Finnish for Willow, took the time to share her deepest thoughts and wishes with me. It is now my time to honor her, courtesy of these words.

I shall always be grateful for the connection that we forged, knowing that the mutual love we shared was *the limitless, bottomless feeling of welcoming with gratitude everything that life has to offer* kind of love, if I may cite her directly.

As spoken by the Dalai Lama, *the highest happiness is when one reaches the stage of liberation, at which there is no more suffering.*

May you now enjoy this time of much earned liberation, my dearest Raita.

Personal Message

It is in becoming aware of the Oneness of all life that we are able to more fully experience the inter-connectivity that we all share. This, in turn, leads each to recognize that all have a responsibility to control, and ultimately eliminate, the negative forces that bring discord, suffering and unhappiness to the forefront.

How is this accomplished?

By focusing one's energies on that which they wish to attract more of into their lives, which ultimately comes down to changing the way one thinks, feels and acts toward themselves and others.

As the spark of Divine Love begins to flame within each individual soul, it grows in both intensity and magnitude until it completely embraces that which is life.

It becomes one's birthright, henceforth, to be happy, and, in so doing, to seek to provide an atmosphere of peace, joy and devotion (service) towards all life, including the animal kingdom, plant kingdom and mineral kingdom.

The Ultimate Enlightenment For 2012

It is in performing even the humblest of tasks that we begin to come to the realization that we are promoting not only our own spiritual advancement, but that of others as well. It is in doing so that the whole of Creation triumphs.

If I may cite a few words attributed to Mahatma Ghandi, *God has no religion*. In essence, this means that we must be the change we wish to see in the world.

It cannot be put any more succinctly than this.

Yin Yang symbol

Author's Note

When you are truly inspired by some great purpose, some extraordinary project ... your mind transcends its limitations, your consciousness expands in every direction, and you find yourself in a new, great and wonderful world. Then those dormant forces, faculties and talents inside you become alive, and you discover yourself to be a greater person by far than you ever dreamed yourself to be.

These words, attributed to Patanjali, the compiler of the *Yoga Sutras*, a book about the spiritual man possibly dated to the second century BC, so resonate with me that I felt it important to denote them herein. Once experienced, this feeling of transcendence cannot be forgotten.

Officially begun on May 3, 2006, which would have been the 70th birthday of my deceased father, *The Ultimate Enlightenment For 2012: All We Need Is Ourselves*, was released as an e-publication on July 13, 2007.

This is its first release in paperback form.

Dedicated to the memory of John Lennon, it is possible to *imagine* a loving world.

The Ultimate Enlightenment For 2012

A world where competition, greed, envy, hatred and jealousy have been banished in our efforts to create a world where people live together in peace and harmony, *sharing all the world*, for it is in creating a brotherhood of humanity, that the world *will be as one*.

As we venture into the realm of the unknown, this is the mission that we have been entrusted with.

I wish to denote a special thanks to my dear Aussie friend, Brian McFarlane, for sharing his penned poem (refer to page 127) with me.

A special thank you is extended to Mônica Fadul from Uberlândia, Minas Gerais, Brazil, for granting me the privilege of using her photograph, *Love Is All There Is*, as the cover image.

Feel free to view her magnificent visual collection online at http://www.flickr.com/photos/nika_fadul/

I also wish to extend heartfelt thanks to authors Reverend Dr. Michael Beckwith, Nick Bunick, Joseph Campbell, Dave Droar, Michael Gelb, Esther and Jerry Hicks, Jean Claude Koven, Eileen Nauman, Jon Peniel, Robert Rabbin, James Arthur Ray and Ethan Walker III, all of whom are quoted herein with full citation.

The Ultimate Enlightenment For 2012

I am now directing one and all to take the time to check out the FREE HUGS campaign online video [1] whereby you can expect to feel that swell within your very soul.

This is the real life controversial story of Juan Mann. His sole mission was to reach out and hug a stranger in order to brighten up their life. In this cited video, Juan reminds me of John Lennon.

In this age of social dis-connectivity and lack of human contact, the effects of the FREE HUGS campaign were phenomenal. As this symbol of human hope began to spread across the city, police and officials ordered the FREE HUGS campaign *banned*.

What we then witness is the true spirit of humanity coming together in what can only be described as awe inspiring.

For additional information, one can also take the time to visit the official home of the FREE HUGS campaign. [2]

---

[1] http://www.youtube.com/watch?v=vr3x_RRJdd4
[2] http://www.freehugscampaign.org/

Reviews

This is a book to help readers *satisfy those inner longings for spirituality*.

Feelings we long for that so often seem elusive need not be, for it is through deep inner awareness that this author shows us how it is simply right here all the time.

With no special ritual, nor any need to acknowledge 'this God over that God,' Michele Doucette recognizes that spirituality is already programmed into every gene of our bodies. It is not 'out there' somewhere, but here within.

I highly recommend this book as a *deeply moving read* that is sure to make you pause and feel the peace ripple through your soul.

– Suzanne Olsson, author of *Jesus In Kashmir, The Lost Tomb* and co-author of *Roza Bal: The Tomb of Jesus*

The Ultimate Enlightenment For 2012

This book is written with both *strength and passion* for the very subjects contained within. A student of spirituality and alternative beliefs, the reading of this book served to open my eyes.

A *must read* for anyone trying to find their true inner self, with many online references that further compliment the writing.

Thank you for taking the time to write a book that has helped guide me along my path in the universe.

– Shawn Foubert, student of Massage Therapy

The Ultimate Enlightenment For 2012

The concept that each one of us has the power to affect the direction of humanity is not new, but has quite often been misinterpreted. Michele Doucette brings a *fresh approach* to the question of how we can step into our *soul purpose* and help create *a better world*.

We often forget that we are *spiritual beings partaking in a physical adventure*. Our lives focus on the need to succeed in business or the pursuit of fame and fortune. We can also become caught up in the mundane pleasures, easily seduced by the misuse of power, whereby the gratification of our earthly goals blinds us to our innate potential to aid one another and to acknowledge that we are all connected.

If one suffers, we all undergo adversity. If one finds joy, we are all uplifted.

Michele quotes John Lennon in her acknowledgments. Also borrowing from the inspiring words of that gifted individual, I would suggest that you read this book so that you, too, can be motivated to *shine on*.

– Marion Webb-De Sisto, author of *Crystal Skulls: Emissaries of Healing and Sacred Wisdom*

Michele Doucette takes you by the hand and introduces you to your best friend: yourself. Gently, clearly and precisely, she weaves many roads together, showing that while the paths are many, there is really only one dance of which we are all partners. What an exciting time to live and make a difference!

Backing up her statements, Michele provides excellent websites for reference and support. Herein, *the path is well lit* for each individual who is ready to change prior patterns. In the twinkling of an eye, we are evolving and growing into our changing perspective for our Galactic Citizenship.

Life is an ever changing point of view and Michele points out how we are at a convergence of space and matter. She also highlights the importance of emotions in the creation of each individual's frame of reference.

The Ultimate Enlightenment For 2012 is a *must have* in every Health Practitioner's reference library, written simply to be understood by everyone.

– Joelle Houze, author of *Touching the Life Force* and *Dancing With God*

The Ultimate Enlightenment For 2012

I was recently honored with the experience of reading *The Ultimate Enlightenment For 2012*. A very captivating and easy read, I also found it to be *extremely interesting, thought provoking* and *enlightening*.

Compiled at the end of each chapter are useful websites that one can visit, all of which further expound on the written information. It was incredible to see how much research went into the writing of this book as well as the incredibly broad knowledge base from which it came.

This is a book *well worth reading*. Not only has Michele provided a book with a broad platform and much to learn from and ponder, but she has also provided *a springboard for infinite learning*.

We also have the treat of soaking up information, thoughts and perspectives Michele has so eloquently presented. In addition, by including so many useful and pertinent links to follow, she leads us to areas which enable us to personally gather more wisdom, different perspectives and expanded knowledge. Thank you, Michele, for such a wonderful book.

– Genn Waite, owner/operator of Arkansas Crystal Works

The Ultimate Enlightenment For 2012

Michele Doucette has come up with a winner of a book here, *writing what it is that many of us are experiencing* in this New Age. More and more people are searching everywhere for what is inside of their own being.

This book reminds me of the television commercials where someone could have had a V8 – *a book of truths*, right under your nose, you read it and voila, clarification to a max.

When I finished reading this book, there was a calm deep within me. My spirit and soul were as one with the universe and I felt like I make a difference in this world.

We are all here to make a difference and Michele offers each and every one of us many references and roads to travel in order to reach our final destination.

A keeper of a book, I hope that Michele continues to write and share her insights and wisdom, teaching us for many years to come.

– Maria Breau Yoppolo, MLS

The Ultimate Enlightenment For 2012

We live in troubled times where people are seeking the truth, trying to understand their relationship with God and their purpose in life.

Michele has done a wonderful job in allowing her reading audience to benefit from the tremendous concepts that she shares.

I was very grateful that Michele had included portions from my book, *In God's Truth*, along with the thoughts of other spiritual authors that I admire and respect. She should be applauded for both the tremendous research she has done as well as her ability to tie together these various concepts and thoughts into a *coherent and inspiring work*.

This book is an absolute *must read* for every person that is on a spiritual quest to understand the truth and walk in God's light.

Thank you, Michele, for leading us to that light.

– Nick Bunick, author of *In God's Truth* and the subject of *The Messengers: A True Story of Angelic Presence and the Return to the Age of Miracles*

The Ultimate Enlightenment For 2012

Reading has been my hobby since I first learned to read, and for the last thirty plus years I have indulged in reading spiritual books. I am now at the point where very few books catch my interest and hold it because either they offer very little in terms of innovative thoughts or because they are very verbose and yet say very little.

This book is *one of those rare books* that captures your attention from the beginning, expanding your appreciation as you keep on reading. While some of the material is not new, Michele is able to weave a golden path that heightens the reader's understanding, giving them something to contemplate at the end.

The many links that she offers, thereby enabling the reader to dig deeper, should that be their choice, are exceptional with today's wonderful potential of the internet.

I strongly recommend this book to those who are interested in the spiritual path as well as those who just desire to know where we, as humans, are directed.

Congratulations Michele, you did an excellent job.

– Elio Serra, USA

The Ultimate Enlightenment For 2012

Michele Doucette has written a *most powerful message of liberation for mankind* living at the beginning of the 21st century.

This work can be a life altering view into the consciousness of humanity, into the consciousness of ourselves, thereby empowering each of us to be the co-creators of our own unique universe.

What is written in this book must be understood by any person who wishes to make the transition rapidly coming to our planet. Contained throughout this work are many, many resources for further exploration and reinforcement of the truths remarkable set forth in this well written and conceived document.

Thanks to the talent of writers like Michele who can bring together a myriad of sources from diverse backgrounds, more minds, perhaps your mind, may be reached with the truths she so eloquently lays before us.

With works like this one, perhaps not far from now, we will see the truth begin spreading and filling our world, lighting the lamp for all to see.

The Ultimate Enlightenment For 2012

On a more personal note, I wished that I had this resource tool in my possession when my own world was once filled with fear and confusion. I think that many, many days of searching and pain might have been avoided with the knowledge contained within this book.

Bravo, Michele! You are keeping the home light burning. Our world is better because of your work. I am looking forward to more of the same in the time to come.

On behalf of the world, I say thank you.

– David Shirk, USA

The Ultimate Enlightenment For 2012

All We Need Is Ourselves is a phrase that has been expressed through time by many spiritual teachers. Many times the text is so esoteric that it has been hard for many to grasp.

One element that stands out in Michele's writing style is that *her words are infused with her heart energy and passion* for reaching out to others, like she is talking to you, one on one.

Having compiled extensive information from other sources, she has integrated them together into *a very pleasurable reading experience.*

The subjects she has chosen to showcase in this work touched upon many questions and issues that I have been working on.

Michele, your energy infused into this book radiates your path as a teacher, making all clear and approachable.

I highly recommend this book to other seekers.

– Linda Frisch, USA

The Ultimate Enlightenment For 2012: All We Need Is Ourselves makes an *excellent read* that is *very enlightening.*

This book is *straight to the point*, addressing all kinds of spiritual issues surrounding 2012. Many important issues are touched upon in this book and Michele has gathered *some of the best resources* surrounding the New Earth phenomenon, integrating them into this book.

I highly recommend this book to anyone wanting to learn more about the future and their place in it.

– Jason Randhawa, WhatIsMetaphysics.com

The Ultimate Enlightenment For 2012

An *excellent tool* for anyone who wants to know about moving into a new paradigm shift during these coming days.

Michele Doucette has written *a brilliant perspective of a spiritual road map*, providing the reader with websites and quotes that all can explore. This book is *indicative of both her thirst for knowledge and the application of such* to change her life. Included is a most tremendous bibliography worth delving into.

I highly recommend this *noteworthy book* to the spiritual seeker.

– Bettye Johnson, author of *Secrets of the Magdalene Scrolls: The Forbidden Truth of the Life and Times of Mary Magdalene* and its sequel *Mary Magdalene, Her Legacy* as well as *Awakening the Genie Within*

The Ultimate Enlightenment For 2012

At last there is a meaningful answer to the question I am asked by countless people who want to learn more about their true nature … "Where do I start?"

Michele Doucette provides an easy to follow roadmap in this delightful book, *The Ultimate Enlightenment For 2012: All We Need Is Ourselves*. She lovingly holds the reader's hand as she takes them along on her journey of self discovery.

This book is a *veritable goldmine of resources*, liberally sprinkled with references and links to exceptional websites. Anyone reading her insights and following the path she so clearly defines will emerge richer and far more empowered for the experience.

As Michele points out, this is a journey that we all will ultimately have to make. Taking your first steps back into the infinite mystery cannot be any easier than following in Michele's footsteps.

– Jean-Claude Koven, author of *Going Deeper: How to Make Sense of Your Life When Your Life Makes No Sense*

The Ultimate Enlightenment For 2012

Michele, you did a great job writing this book. It certainly *builds the case for one to awaken*. I found that it confirmed all the knowledge and beliefs that I hold true.

While you certainly said it all, the only thing that I would continue to emphasize would be *the power of intent*. I have become convinced that *intent is the most important element in manifestation*.

I am so very fortunate in as much as I recently found the "stillness within." Once found, one guards against ever losing it. Hopefully, each of your readers will, one day, be rewarded in the same way.

You are deeply blessed and loved for both spreading the light and for being who you are becoming.

– Richard Guertin, USA

What a most amazing job you have done in bringing these inspired sources together, all in such an easy to read book that just flows. There is *so much food for thought* to be found here.

There were several passages that deeply resonated with me: [1] Prayers are always answered, [2] Monitor your thoughts carefully, being sure only to think about what you want, because the universe will take a snapshot of your thoughts for manifestation purposes, [3] In essence, we are becoming a new species of Light, a new vibrational being, [4] During this time, we can only imagine what full activation of our DNA will allow us to accomplish for Planetary healing and restoration, [5] In every moment, we have the opportunity to contract or expand our awareness, [6] There are many paths to the top of the mountain but there is only one summit, which is love.

My dear friend, I thoroughly enjoyed reading this book and am looking forward to reading others that you have written and/or shall write. You are *such an inspiration* to me.

– Suzi Cullen, Australia

The Ultimate Enlightenment For 2012

Michele has drawn together *a wonderful spectrum of knowledge about the Ascension process* that is unfolding in our time and shared it in a gentle, loving, easy to understand manner. She has woven a tapestry from the many threads of understanding and provides many links for further study and clarification. It is *a tool that will help many* on this path.

– Dr. Richard Presser, author of *The Coming Golden Age and How To Prepare For It*

Prologue

Truth be told, there is nothing inherently different in the messages contained herein for they have been mirrored by countless individuals before my time and will undoubtedly be followed by many thereafter.

The only inherent and reflected difference, however, lies in the manner in which the words have been orchestrated by myself.

There have been many individuals, over the course of these last few years, who have shared that I have been both a catalyst as well as a bearer of information during the times when it was needed most.

If this is the role that I am to serve; then, so too, will I have been successful.

Introduction

The Hopi are a Native American nation who primarily live on a reservation in Arizona, referring to themselves as "The Peaceable People."

In keeping with the ancient Mayan civilization, clearly the most advanced in relation to time-science knowledge, the Hopi believe that we are currently in between the end of the fifth world (completed in 1987) and the beginning of the sixth (to begin in 2012).

The Hopi refer to this time between worlds as the Apocalypse or Revelation, a time of the revealing of truth. It has been foretold that the completion of this "time between worlds" will bring regeneration to the planet in that Mother Earth, a living entity, will transcend to another level (frequency or consciousness) and a new and special era will begin, a time for all things positive. The times are here for total brotherhood.

It should be noted that these adept sky watchers, the ancient Mayans, invented a calendar of remarkable accuracy and complexity, choosing December 21, 2012 as the end of their Long Count calendar.

Accordingly, the Mayan sixth world is actually blank, meaning that it is up to us, as co-creators, as a human family, to begin creating the new world, the new civilization, that we want *right now*.

Clearly, this is an important time for us to work through issues, both individually and collectively.

The Hopi and Mayan elders do not prophesy that everything will come to an end, but that this is merely a time of transition from one world age to another.

As my friend Michael Haupt has written in response to whether or not we are living in End Times, the answer is both yes and no.

No, I do not believe that the current global situation means an imminent end of the world, the doomsday scenario so many teach and believe. Yes, we are reaching the end of an age. We are on the cusp of a new age. So, we are currently experiencing the necessary changes and shifts before the new age can commence.

Michael is not the only person saying the same thing. Gregg Braden, author of *The God Code*, is the most recognized person currently engaged in both evaluating and revealing the scientific phenomena pointing to this shift.

The Ultimate Enlightenment For 2012

It has also been stated that in 2012 the plane of our solar system will line up exactly with the plane of our galaxy, the Milky Way, a cycle that has taken 26,000 years to complete.

While an explanation of the Mayan calendar lies outside the confines of this publication, there are many websites that may be of interest to the reader. I have taken the time to list but a few.

<u>The How and Why of The Mayan End Date In 2012 AD</u> [3]

<u>Foundation for the Law of Time</u> (José Argüelles) [4]

<u>The Mayan Prophecy of 2012</u> [5]

<u>13 Moon Natural Time Calendar</u> [6]

<u>All About 2012</u> [7]

<u>Beyond 2012</u> [8]

---

[3] http://edj.net/mc2012/Why2012.html
[4] http://www.lawoftime.org/
[5] http://www.13moon.com/prophecy%20page.htm
[6] http://www.13moon.com/
[7] http://www.greatdreams.com/2012.htm
[8] http://www.diagnosis2012.co.uk/1.htm

The Ultimate Enlightenment For 2012

2012 Links [9]

Sunset Stonehenge

---

[9] http://www.diagnosis2012.co.uk/link.htm

Inner Rumblings

All beings, be it in this current lifetime or in a future lifetime, will embark on a spiritual journey. Such is the natural progression of what it means to be human.

When an individual begins seeking answers to questions such as

Who am I?

Why am I here?

What is my purpose?

then he/she is resonating with soul knowingness, cognizant of the fact that the journey of liberation and destination has begun, for it is this very questioning that drives one towards awakening. Quite simply, you become a seeker of your own truth, the truth that already exists within.

These opening and most pertinent questions soon lead to a multitude of others as one delves into related issues such as free will, karma, predestination and the inner knowledge of having predetermined the fulfillment of one's purpose, to name but a few.

Both Jesus and Buddha taught that love means compassion, kindness, caring, giving, sharing and harmlessness. All of these components collectively add up to what is referred to as unselfish love being the way, despite their disagreement over names and/or particulars.

The universal spirit, rather than being an individual per sé, comprises, and is, all things in the entire universe, together as one. This energy, this essence, this life force, includes us, includes nature, includes the very universe itself. It also has a consciousness, which is incomprehensible from a left brain (logical, analytical, objective) point of view.

As one begins to expand their spiritual consciousness, they begin to realize that there is more to life, and the universe, than meets the eye simply because creation is too astounding and phenomenal to be deemed haphazard.

There is a oneness that pervades everything.

As your spiritual consciousness continues to grow, you find yourself understanding the underlying connection of everything, until you eventually arrive at the realization that others are actually part of you, that you are a part of them, that all are one.

Upon realizing this actualization, you also feel, and manifest, unselfish love (denoted previously as compassion, kindness, caring, giving, sharing and harmlessness). These are the values, the earmarks of true spirituality, taking us back to both Jesus and Buddha.

When such a spiritual change takes place within you, everyone you come into contact with will, indeed, be better off having known you, for they, too, will have the ability to change, and spread the beauty of unselfish love to others.

Like multiple ripples in a pond that are created from the throwing of just one rock, this unselfish love makes you a physical vehicle for the universal spirit, as it moves through you, and thus throughout the world.

Jon Peniel states that "when you become enlightened, you are very, very busy helping others to attain the same freedom, peace, and unselfish love you have found, or you go on and ascend to a higher vibrational plane." [10]

---

[10] Peniel, Jon. (1997). *The Children of the Law of One and The Lost Teachings of Atlantis* (p 37). Alamosa, CO: Network.

If you elect to stay, "you *work* for the universal spirit, so to speak. You align your will, with universal will, and thus you become very busy doing your little part in the *universal flow*." [11]

According to the teachings of the Atlantean Children of the Law of One, "universal principles dictate that the kind of world you live in, and the creation of your future world, is all up to you. It is entirely your choice, and in your power to change, all by just making changes in yourself." [12]

Quite clearly, Peniel is speaking here of the Law of Attraction.

The Law of Attraction is a universal reality, meaning, quite simply, that we attract into our lives that which we focus on and give power (energy) to, whether it be negative (fear, anger, worry, stress, hate) or positive (love, peace of mind, health, well-being, wealth, success, happiness).

You can fully expect that there will be many trials and tribulations as you change inside to become a better person, but ultimately it will be done, if it is your will to do so.

---

[11] Peniel, Jon. (1997). *The Children of the Law of One and The Lost Teachings of Atlantis* (p 37). Alamosa, CO: Network.
[12] Ibid, pp 41-42.

The Ultimate Enlightenment For 2012

The world outside you will change according to the changes you make within yourself.

As Michael Gelb shares, "seekers must cultivate the ability to listen and look within." [13]

Given my personal belief in reincarnation, I believe that once we learn to master something in a previous life, as in manifesting, it is not lost to us. We are the ones who choose to bring these talents with us when we decide to move into a new life experience.

Attracting abundance is knowledge. As with any skill, how good you are at it depends on how efficient you have become at performing it.

Those people who are efficient in attracting by way of the Law of Attraction have trained their minds to focus on that which they desire. Abundance comes to them naturally, without even realizing how they do it.

---

[13] Gelb, Michael. (2004). *Da Vinci Decoded: Discovering the Spiritual Principles of Leonardo's Seven Principles* (p 48). New York, NY: Delacorte Press.

The Ultimate Enlightenment For 2012

Broken Manacles

The Power of Thought

Buddha understood this universal law when he stated that *we are shaped by our thoughts*, thereby becoming what we think. Regardless of whether or not you believe it, your beliefs, your feelings, your thoughts, control your destiny.

Whatever we do, we do to ourselves. There is a law of karma that says one reaps what one sows, be it by way of thoughts, feelings, intentions or actions. This, in and of itself, should offer compelling spiritual reflection, most imperative for self-examination, given that we are the creators of our own misery.

Beliefs have a dominant and powerful effect on every aspect of one's life.

History tells us that there have been individuals and powerful institutions, all willing to kill, based on the prevailing beliefs of the time. It is even more shocking, in the twenty-first century, to realize that this mentality still exists. It is for this crucial reason that each individual needs to scrutinize the beliefs that are held true, because of what they create in their own lives.

What, then, should we believe for the greatest good?

As taken from *The Children of the Law of One and The Lost Teachings of Atlantis*,[14] a fine example follows.

→ Do your beliefs further the manifestations of unselfish love, or inhibit the manifestations of unselfish love?

→ Do they breed anger, hatred and harm or tranquility, love and healing?

→ Do they make for a better life, or a worse life?

→ Do they make for a better world for others, or a worse world?

We live in a world that has created the illusion of separateness from the universal spirit. This, in and of itself, has become the basis for the creation of selfishness.

When one takes the time to ask such questions [15] as ...

→ How much harm has been done in the names of God, country or tribe?

---

[14] Peniel, Jon. (1997). *The Children of the Law of One and The Lost Teachings of Atlantis* (p 61). Alamosa, CO: Network.
[15] Ibid.

→ How much horror and pain has been inflicted because someone has a different racial, national, tribal, class, or religious belief?

… such is indicative that one is *truly on the path* which, ultimately, leads to spiritual enlightenment.

As shared further by Peniel, "those who know not that they are one, act not as one. Those who act not as one, create not love, but suffering and disharmony. What you create, you receive." [16]

In essence, the fruits of your acts will follow your days. Once again, we are speaking of karma.

Such is an apt descriptor of what Peniel calls 'separate consciousness'.

He goes further to share that when we talk about the state of a person's consciousness, "we are essentially talking about the state of their awareness of the world around them …

---

[16] Peniel, Jon. (1997). *The Children of the Law of One and The Lost Teachings of Atlantis* (p 63). Alamosa, CO: Network.

directly related to the way they view, interpret, understand, and interact with, everyone and everything around them." [17]

A person's point of view, therefore, is affected by "both the state of their consciousness, and their beliefs and programming. Beliefs and programming are usually in sync with a person's level of consciousness. However, consciousness is dominant, and if there is a shift to a higher or lower state, the new consciousness can alter and override a person's beliefs and programming in order to match the new level of consciousness." [18]

Taking it one important step further, "the fact is, all things in the Universe are essentially made of the same 'stuff', and are totally interdependent and connected. So we cannot be truly separate from the rest of the Universe, we can only be a 'part' of it all. But we can think we are separate. We can believe we are separate. And then we act like we are separate. Having separate self consciousness doesn't mean that you are really separate, but it does mean having a total 'illusion' of separateness from everyone and everything else in the Universe. And when a person truly believes they are

---

[17] Peniel, Jon. (1997). *The Children of the Law of One and The Lost Teachings of Atlantis* (p 65). Alamosa, CO: Network.
[18] Ibid.

separate, they naturally focus on themselves. And when someone believes they are separate, and they focus their attention, and their energy, on their self, this naturally leads to selfishness. This is the BIG issue, the BIG problem of all problems; the only REAL problem. As silly and simple as it sounds, it is serious - simple selfishness is the root of all problems and evils that exist on Earth. This is one of the greatest, most important teachings to understand." [19]

The ego, or sense of being separate, "is the knowledge of good and evil. In order for something to be good or evil there must be an individual I to reference as the subject of good and evil. In other words good and evil are relative only to the individual ego. The ego doesn't want us looking for God because when we find God, the illusion of being an ego will be destroyed. One cannot see God and continue to live as a separate person. Each and every day we will watch the mind carefully and destroy our divisiveness. We will stop

---

[19] Peniel, Jon. (1997). *The Children of the Law of One and The Lost Teachings of Atlantis* (pp 67-68). Alamosa, CO: Network.

separating and start uniting. We will stop hating and start loving." [20]

The only cure for evil, suffering, and all problems that we are faced with in today's world lies in losing our separate consciousness and selfishness by regaining consciousness of our oneness with everything.

This can only be attained through unselfish love, looking to both Jesus and Buddha as important and living examples of compassion, kindness, caring, giving, sharing and harmlessness.

We must see the illusions of self consciousness that we carry with us in our mind and break them.

This is why I see this time as being a very exciting time.

In knowing that we create our own reality by the very thoughts that we think, the very words that we verbalize, the very actions that we employ, now is the time to learn to let go of fear and concentrate solely on the expansion of love and forgiveness.

---

[20] Walker III, Ethan. (2003). *The Mystic Christ: The Light of Non-Duality and the Path of Love According to the Life and Teachings of Jesus* (p 49). Norman, OK: Devi Press Inc.

The Ultimate Enlightenment For 2012

In working with thought forms, stay positive. It is only in thinking positive thoughts that we continue to attract more positive people and positive events/happenings into our lives.

In this way we become like the ripples in the pond, creating a domino of positive effects in the world.

On the flip side, the more we focus on the negative, the depressed, the dismal ... the more negativity we bring into our life. Clearly, we must become more aware of our thoughts in order to eliminate the unnecessary negative or judgmental ones.

It is for this very reason that I no longer watch the news on TV, read magazines or listen to the radio. I have eliminated all media negativity in my life for the simple reason that I was finding myself existing in a state of depression, unable to focus on the joys associated with life and living.

In keeping with the changes that we are trying to bring forth within, it is important to remember that for every action or non-action, there is a consequence. When we give our minds and our responsibility away, we give our lives away. Is this what we really want?

It is important to become aware that most of the media is controlled by just a few.

The Ultimate Enlightenment For 2012

Take the time to use discernment.

Look for the hidden agenda (as has been summarized in the following bullets as per David Icke).

→ Why is this information being presented to you?

→ What is their "real" agenda?

→ Is it a case of problem-reaction-solution?

→ Do "they" create a problem so that "we" react and ask for a fix?

→ Do "they" then offer a solution?

→ Is the "solution" what "they" really wanted in the first place?

The real power lies with the many, not the few. Do not allow yourself to be fooled. Infinite power exists within every individual.

We have the power to decide our own destiny, but only if we do not give that power away.

When something happens that we do not like, we have a tendency to look for someone else to blame.

When there is a problem in the world, we wonder what *they* are going to do about it. Clearly, this non-action has resulted in the giving away of our power.

The few want to control your mind because when they have succeeded in doing that, they have you; hence, the answer lies in taking the mind back, thinking for ourselves and allowing others to do the same without condemnation or ridicule.

We create our own reality by our thoughts and actions. If we change our thoughts and actions we *will* change the world. It really is that simple.

More people are waking up to the fact that, in making these necessary and needed thought changes, the citizens of Earth are allowing their own frequencies, which may be in the form of directed energy, invocations, prayers, meditations, activations and/or consciousness, to draw more love and light to the planet and its inhabitants.

In this sense, a true co-creation is occurring whereby Heaven is coming to Earth and Earth is rising up to Heaven. In this sense, it is not just a top down frequency raising, it is also a raising upward, a true melding of humanity and divinity.

Much of what has been shared, thus far, is, in essence, what has recently come to be known as *The Secret*, courtesy of Rhonda Byrne, creator of the DVD.

Brought to the television world by Oprah on February 8, 2007, the show was aptly entitled **What Is The Secret?**

This has been the only Oprah show, known to date, that has skyrocketed her ratings through the roof. Guests included Reverend Dr. Michael Beckwith, Rhonda Byrne, Jack Canfield, Lisa Nichols and James Arthur Ray.

Rhonda Byrne says that following the philosophy associated with the Law of Attraction will enable you to create the life that you want. Following the research trail, she traced the idea of The Secret back to 3500 BC. [21]

A follow-up reaction show, entitled **The Secret Is Out: A Huge Reaction**, aired one week later, with Reverend Dr. Michael Beckwith and James Arthur Ray returning as guests.

---

[21] Byrne, Rhonda. (2007). *What Is The Secret?* Retrieved February 9, 2007 from http://www2.oprah.com/spiritself/slide/20070208/ss_200702 08_284_101.jhtml

The Ultimate Enlightenment For 2012

Michael says that "to begin living the ultimate life that you want, you must first describe that life in as much detail as possible." [22]

This is not an exercise whereby one merely lists the ways that they would like their present circumstances to change. Instead, one must really think about how they want their life to be.

It is Michael who suggested the following affirmation: "I see myself living a life [in which] I am absolutely, totally healthy. Everything is working together for my good. There is prosperity flowing through me. I am in a place of employment that I really love. I am really providing value everywhere I go." [23]

James continued what Michael was saying by adding that it is this describing, not asking, not hoping, that is just the first step which he calls intention. "After you have established your intention, the next step is attention. Here, you should

---

[22] Beckwich, Reverend Dr. Michael. (2007). *The Secret Is Out: A Huge Reaction*. Retrieved February 17, 2007 from http://www2.oprah.com/spiritself/slide/20070216/ss_200702 16_284_101.jhtml

[23] Ibid.

feel gratitude and maintain this feeling that your intended goals are coming." [24]

The third step involves taking action. "This is the scary part, even when you teach this stuff," James says. "Step forward, taking action in the direction ... not where you are currently, but moving forward and saying, 'Okay, if this is who I am becoming, then what action would I take right now if I were already there?' " [25]

Past teachers of *The Secret* are noted as having been Ludwig von Beethoven, Alexander Graham Bell, Buddha, Joseph Campbell, Andrew Carnegie, Winston Churchill, Robert Collier, Thomas Edison, Albert Einstein, Ralph Waldo Emerson, Henry Ford, Victor Hugo, Carl Jung, Martin Luther King, Isaac Newton, Plato, W. Clement Stone and Hermes Trismegistus.

---

[24] Ray, James Arthur. (2007). *The Secret Is Out: A Huge Reaction*. Retrieved February 17, 2007 from http://www2.oprah.com/spiritself/slide/20070216/ss_200702 16_284_101.jhtml
[25] Ibid.

The Ultimate Enlightenment For 2012

Current teachers are shared as being ......

John Assaraf – Entrepreneur (a former street kid) [26]

Reverend Dr. Michael Beckwith – Visionary [27]

Lee Brower – Teacher [28]

Jack Canfield – Author [29]

John F. Demartini – Philosopher (told he was Learning Disabled) [30]

Marie Diamond – Feng Shui Consultant [31]

Mike Dooley – Writer [32]

Bob Doyle – Author [33]

---

[26] http://www.johnassaraf.com
[27] http://www.agapelive.com
[28] http://www.quadrantliving.com
[29] http://www.jackcanfield.com
[30] http://www.drdemartini.com
[31] http://www.mariediamond.com
[32] http://www.tut.com
[33] http://www.wealthbeyondreason.com

The Ultimate Enlightenment For 2012

Hale Dwoskin – The Sedona Method [34]

Morris E. Goodman – The Miracle Man [35]

John Gray – Psychologist [36]

John Hagelin – Quantum Physicist [37]

Bill Harris – Therapist [38]

Esther Hicks – The Teachings of Abraham [39]

Ben Johnson – Physician [40]

Lisa Nichols – Author [41]

Bob Proctor – Philosopher [42]

---

[34] http://www.sedona.com
[35] http://www.themiracleman.org
[36] http://www.marsvenus.com
[37] http://www.hagelin.org
[38] http://www.centerpointe.com
[39] http://www.abraham-hicks.com
[40] http://www.thehealingcode.com/sindex.html
[41] http://www.lisa-nichols.com
[42] http://www.bobproctor.com

The Ultimate Enlightenment For 2012

James Arthur Ray – Philosopher [43]

David Schirmer – Investment Trainer [44]

Marci Shimoff – Author [45]

Joe Vitale – Metaphysician (was homeless 20 years ago) [46]

Denis Waitley – Psychologist [47]

Fred Alan Wolf – Quantum Physicist [48]

In addition to these teachers, I have managed to locate other websites, all in keeping with the power of thought, that are very much worth exploring.

Creating Your Own Reality and The Power of Thought [49]

Do You Make These Law of Attraction Blunders? [50]

---

[43] http://www.jamesray.com/index.php
[44] http://www.tradingedge.com.au
[45] http://www.marcishimoff.com
[46] http://www.mrfire.com
[47] http://www.waitley.com
[48] http://www.fredalanwolf.com
[49] http://www.soul-awakening.com/philosophy/creating-your-own-reality.htm
[50] http://www.selfgrowth.com/articles/Doyle14.html

The Ultimate Enlightenment For 2012

Gateway To The Soul: September 2005 [51]

The Power of Thought [52]

The Power of Your Thoughts [53]

The Silent Power of Thought [54]

Thought Power: Sri Swami Sivananda [55]

Your Very Existence Depends On The Law of Attraction [56]

---

[51] http://www.portalsofspirit.com/GatewaySept2005.htm
[52] http://www.meilach.com/spiritual/books/wisdomoframadahn/chapter4.htm
[53] http://hinduwebsite.com/selfdevt/thought_power.asp
[54] http://www.worldspirituality.org/power-of-thought.html
[55] http://www.dlshq.org/download/thought_power.htm
[56] http://www.wizardwonderland.com/loa.htm

The Ultimate Enlightenment For 2012

Anything you want, you got it.

Anything you need, you got it.

Anything at all, you got it.

~ Roy Orbison ~

There are no accidents

or coincidences in this world.

Nothing is by chance.

Everything you experience

is a direct manifestation

of where you focus your attention

and how you hold your bodymind's vibration.

~ Jafree Oswald ~

author of *How To Raise Your Manifesting Vibration*

Prayers Are Always Answered

Everyone lives in the world of his or her thoughts. Thoughts are energy; hence, positive thoughts attract positive results, naturally, while negative thoughts attract negative results. Like attracts like.

Let's face it, we tend to hang around people who are like us, people who think the way we think. Our thoughts, beliefs, expectations, words and actions create a magnetic field around us that attracts to us people and situations that match our energy and our vibration. It cannot be put any more succinctly than that.

We create our own reality. We attract those things in our life (money, relationships, employment) that we focus on. Even though it is not as simple as stating an affirmation, no affirmation is going to work if your mind (thought) is negating the positive. When we focus on having less, this is exactly what we create for ourselves.

In this regard, know what you want. Monitor your thoughts carefully, being sure to only think about what you want, because the universe will take a snapshot of your thoughts for manifestation purposes.

The Ultimate Enlightenment For 2012

Make what you want your *burning* desire, your major purpose, for it will be these very thoughts that shall manifest in form. Remain determined to see them fully realized, for success comes to those who have success consciousness.

What shows up in your life has less to do with where you were born, how you were raised or what you look like, and more to do with what you focus on. You get what you think about, what you focus on, what you talk about and what you believe.

Prayer can involve many forms; namely,

→ a visualization (using the power of your mind and the energy of the universe to create what you want in your life)

→ non-discursive meditation (quiet your inner speech and listen, accomplished by saying one thing over and over again)

→ unfocused discursive meditation (witness the flow of inner thoughts without controlling them, allowing the internal conversation to take its course)

→ focused discursive meditation (make a deliberate attempt to narrow down and focus the inner speech)

→ the form of a mantra (a religious syllable or poem, typically from the Sanskrit language)

→ the form of an affirmation (the declaration that something is true which is a form of autosuggestion)

→ expressed as a song

→ the use of prayer beads

→ the use of a prayer wheel

→ a matter of letting go and letting God (putting one's faith in a higher power, knowing that all needs will be taken care of)

Ultimately, it is a belief system based on thought and action.

To become peace in action, one must be peace.

To become love in action, one must be love.

To become forgiveness in action, one must be forgiveness.

As stated in the previous section, we create our own reality through thoughts and actions. If we change our thoughts and actions, we will change the world.

This is all affiliated with prayer, is it not?

Affirmations and positive self talk, along with visualizing, are powerful ways of programming your mind in preparation for success consciousness.

Affirmations are personal statements written in both positive and present tense terms. The more emotion one provokes upon saying these affirmations aloud, the more powerful they become.

Everything is the result of mere thought. This being so, it is the mind that is the builder towards a caring, unselfish and harmless world.

Affirmations are positive statements or directions you make to yourself in order to bring about changes in your subconscious behavior patterns to whatever you will them to be.

Using an affirmation is like "planting a seed in the fertile soil of your sub-conscious mind, and like a seed it needs daily tending or it will die. For this reason, affirmations are tools that are used daily, and frequently, by those who wish to change." [57]

For affirmations to be effective, they must always be stated as positive, already accomplished, results.

Wording them in futuristic terms, such as [1] **I will be**, [2] **I am going to be**, or [3] **I would like to be** actually *prevents the changes* from ever taking place because we are always in the now.

Therefore, giving energy to the positive trait, such as **I am always Unselfishly Loving** always supersedes the negative. (as in **I will become Unselfishly Loving**).

You also need to both *feel* and *mean* the words as you say them, or the affirmation will not be an effective tool.

Creating a visual image to accompany your words is also important.

---

[57] Peniel, Jon. (1997). *The Children of the Law of One and The Lost Teachings of Atlantis* (p 249). Alamosa, CO: Network.

Some people like to create a type of "wish" board whereby they collect an assortment of pictures and/or photographs to represent what they are creating.

When it comes to visualization, I find it incredibly difficult to both see the pictures and try to put myself in the image. It is hard to get emotionally excited about this visualization when all my mind sees is some dark and fuzzy attempts at a new reality.

Not so difficult now that I have discovered Mind Movies, [58] an absolutely phenomenal metaphysical tool.

You know, in all honesty, it really doesn't matter if you cannot visualize very well, as long as you know how to watch videos. Likewise, it really doesn't matter if you cannot raise your emotional vibration easily, as long as you like music.

Mind Movies is a *multi-media tool* that allows you to create a vision of what you want, scored with your favorite song; the one that makes you feel good, the one that makes you want to dance, the one that makes you smile and sing along.

---

[58] http://www.mindmovies.com/?10107

The Ultimate Enlightenment For 2012

In keeping, this allows you to make your *dreams* and *desires* a monumental part of what you *see* and *hear* every day. Watching your Mind Movie every morning and every evening helps you in manifesting through the Law of Attraction.

Gratitude for every aspect of your life that is, and is yet to come, is also one of the keys to the secret of the Law of Attraction.

Too often in our busy lives we forget to be grateful for what we have.

Take the time to stop and appreciate.

Be thankful for your health.

Be thankful for life.

Be thankful for your achievements.

Be thankful for nature.

Be thankful for everyone and everything that contributes to this magnificent and miraculous journey.

Give gratitude.

Feel gratitude.

The Ultimate Enlightenment For 2012

As you become truly appreciative for everything in your life, including those things yet to arrive, you will be truly amazed at how much the feeling of gratitude opens the floodgates of the universe to bring everything to you.

Here are some additional websites worth exploring.

Affirmation Cards: Free Positive Affirmations [59]

Affirmations For Awakening [60]

Count Your Blessings [61]

Gratitude Quotes [62]

Keeping An Attitude of Gratitude [63]

Soulful Living: Gratitude and Giving [64]

---

[59] http://www.vitalaffirmations.com/pool/affirmation-cards.htm
[60] http://www.sun-angel.com/cgi-bin/affirm.pl
[61] http://www.beliefnet.com/index/index_308.html
[62] http://www.beliefnet.com/story/53/story_5396_1.html
[63] http://1stholistic.com/Reading/prose/liv_keeping-an-attitude-of-gratitude.htm
[64] http://www.soulfulliving.com/novemberfeatures.htm

The Ultimate Enlightenment For 2012

Spirit Cards Affirmations [65]

The Power Word Cards [66]

Use Affirmations To Change Your Life [67]

World Prayers [68]

---

[65] http://www.spiritcards.com/affirmations.html
[66] http://www.onwordsupwords.com/onwords2.html
[67] http://www.gems4friends.com/affirmations.html
[68] http://www.worldprayers.org

Spiritual Literacy aka The Spiritual Truth

The only person we can change is ourselves. It is time to begin cleaning out our own hidden closets of wounds and negative attitudes on mental, emotional and spiritual levels.

As we focus on change within, as ripples traverse outward into the realms of the universe, the world comes closer to peace.

To change the consciousness of the world, the first tenant becomes that of focusing on ourselves. Change takes place, one person at a time.

I discovered a very interesting website that spoke of preparing oneself for the global shift that is upon us. It is on this very site that Eileen Nauman speaks of the Vesica Piscis (which rhymes with Jessica Crisis) symbol, an ancient symbol consisting of two overlapping circles that represent the physical world on one side and the spiritual, or causal, world on the other.

It has been further stated that the section where they intersect is the akashic or etheric level, thereby representing the bridge between heaven and earth.

"In the earliest traditions, the supreme being was represented by a sphere, the symbol of a being with no beginning and no end, continually existing, perfectly formed and profoundly symmetrical. The addition of a second sphere represented the expansion of unity into the duality of male and female, god and goddess. By overlapping the two spheres, the god and goddess created a divine offspring. The son or daughter of the god and goddess is associated with the overlapping of the spheres, the resulting three dimensional figure somewhat like an American football." [69]

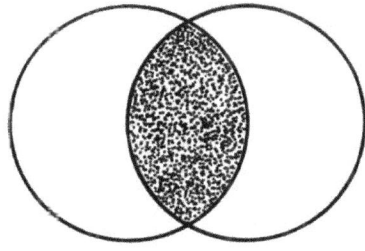

Eileen speaks of utilizing this symbol to help us leap into the New World that we are in the process of creating.

---

[69] Nauman, Eileen. (2006). *Preparing for the Global Shift - Moving to the LIGHT from the DARK: How to Do It*. Retrieved July 13, 2006, from http://www.medicinegarden.com/metaphysics/globalshift2006.html and can be reached at docbones@gotsky.com

The Ultimate Enlightenment For 2012

As such, it can be used to "transcend into peace rather than war, peace rather than chaos, peace rather than hatred and all the lower human emotions," [70] encouraging us to make our own VP symbol using two sixteen feet lengths of yarn.

Given that science was built upon trying something and then repeating the experiment, I strongly suggest that the reader take the time to try this out for themselves.

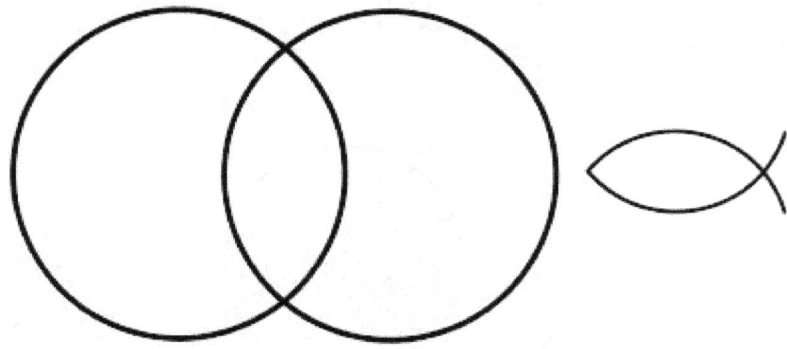

As you can see from the diagram presented on the previous page, the eye of the Vesica Piscis symbol is identical to the symbol used to represent Jesus in Christianity.

---

[70] Nauman, Eileen. (2006). *Preparing for the Global Shift - Moving to the LIGHT from the DARK: How to Do It*. Retrieved July 13, 2006, from http://www.medicinegarden.com/metaphysics/globalshift2006.html and can be reached at docbones@gotsky.com

The Ultimate Enlightenment For 2012

In keeping with the science experiment using the two sixteen feet lengths of yarn, Eileen states that one can test it in a number of ways.

First, step into one of the outer circles, but not into the 'fish' or 'eye' area, being sure to ground yourself. If I may use Eileen's words in this respect, "see silver tree roots gently twining around your ankles and the tip of the root going down through each of your feet and several hundred feet down into Mother Earth." [71]

Close your eyes. Remain within the outer circle for a minute or two and see what happens.

Next, open your eyes and step out of the outer circle. Go to either end of the 'fish' or 'eye' area and step into it.

Once again, ground yourself and close your eyes.

Many people experience many sensations within the eye. Feelings of being pulled forward, pulled backward, pulled to either the left or the right.

---

[71] Nauman, Eileen. (2006). *Preparing for the Global Shift - Moving to the LIGHT from the DARK: How to Do It.* Retrieved July 13, 2006, from http://www.medicinegarden.com/metaphysics/globalshift2006.html and can be reached at docbones@gotsky.com

The Ultimate Enlightenment For 2012

All of this movement adjustment that takes place, according to Eileen, is about "getting your aura or energy field back into balance and harmony." [72]

Once that has been accomplished, be prepared to experience an incredible amount of things.

Possibilities may include seeing a color or two, seeing your Master or Spirit Guide, seeing a loved one who has transitioned, hearing music and/or heightened and accentuated hearing.

What is the point of working within the eye of the VP, you ask?

To use Eileen's words, "this is a way to access our own integration process, clean out our dirty laundry (our wounds, negative emotions) and heal yourself." [73]

In essence, the VP is about opening up and healing.

---

[72] Nauman, Eileen. (2006). *Preparing for the Global Shift - Moving to the LIGHT from the DARK: How to Do It.* Retrieved July 13, 2006, from http://www.medicinegarden.com/metaphysics/globalshift2006.html and can be reached at docbones@gotsky.com
[73] Ibid.

The Ultimate Enlightenment For 2012

The VP can "put you in touch with a special teacher in Spirit. You can receive positive and reinforcing guidance as well. Past lifetimes may unroll like film on a movie screen. The VP, in the finest sense of the word, is a doorway." [74]

To where?

One must sit within this eye in order to determine the answer to this question.

The VP is not "only a doorway, but it is catalytic as well. You cannot sit in the VP and not change for the better. It will accentuate your true, authentic self and bring you to full bloom if you allow it to work with you." [75]

Eileen also shares that when one sits or lies down, making sure their entire body is within the eye, one's aura is adjusted and harmonized.

Once in harmony, the healing begins.

---

[74] Nauman, Eileen. (2006). *Preparing for the Global Shift - Moving to the LIGHT from the DARK: How to Do It.* Retrieved July 13, 2006, from http://www.medicinegarden.com/metaphysics/globalshift2006.html and can be reached at docbones@gotsky.com
[75] Ibid.

The Ultimate Enlightenment For 2012

It has been suggested that one meditate on a daily basis, twenty minute sessions, in the eye of the VP. It would also be advisable to keep a journal of what you feel, hear, see and experience.

When you feel stressed out, upset, angry or losing patience, go sit or lie down in the eye of the VP for five to ten minutes.

Eileen shares that in doing so "all the anger or impatience or feeling out of sorts will simply dissolve away and you will feel strong, steady and in your 'core' being where there is a sense of solidness and peacefulness." [76]

Likewise, you can retreat to this eye when you are anxious, worried, having a panic attack, feeling sick, have a headache, are experiencing arthritis pains.

Clearly, this is where you can turn negative into positive. Separation or duality melds into Oneness. Hurtful emotions move into a feeling of peace and harmony.

---

[76] Nauman, Eileen. (2006). *Preparing for the Global Shift - Moving to the LIGHT from the DARK: How to Do It.* Retrieved July 13, 2006, from http://www.medicinegarden.com/metaphysics/globalshift2006.html and can be reached at docbones@gotsky.com

The VP, then, becomes your very own doorway to the universe.

Is this not a science experiment worth exploring?

Eileen talks about *Warriors for the Light*. Upon reading her article, there were a great many points that resonated with me, which I have chosen to paraphrase from the site.

[1] desiring peace over war

[2] believing that all can live in co-existence without the need for violence

[3] trying not to add to the polluting of the planet

[4] respecting others for their individual belief systems

[5] not allowing themselves to be ruled and controlled by fear

[6] believing and knowing that love and compassion are the real means of achieving peace

[7] working on a daily basis to do at least one good thing for others

[8] not adhering to a victim mentality

The Ultimate Enlightenment For 2012

[9] taking responsibility for their own action choices

[10] understanding that change can only come through the changing of oneself

[11] understanding that harmony and balance must exist within before attempting to help others find the same

[12] detaching themselves from powerful and emotional dramas that drain the life force

[13] practicing compassion (instead of pity or sympathy)

[14] visualizing a world at peace (daily basis)

[15] practicing humility in knowing we are all One

[16] knowing that one's best teacher resides within

[17] respecting all life

[18] respecting all people

[19] understanding that energy can be changed but never destroyed

[20] knowing when to fight, when to retreat, choosing one's battles wisely

The Ultimate Enlightenment For 2012

[21] using anger as a means of transforming it into a pro-active energy

[22] respecting their own inner qualities (no need for envy or jealousy)

[23] always honoring the truth

[24] surrendering only to a higher power

[25] having faith and doing the best they can with life lesson tests

[26] understanding and respecting their individual uniqueness

[27] believing that they are both needed and necessary to help dissolve the Dark

[28] honoring the skills gleaned as a result of personal experiences

[29] treating their body as a temple

[30] treating their body as their partner

[31] possessing a desire to create a new Garden of Eden as a haven for all

Discovering Eileen and her article was a definite case of synchronicity at work.

I encourage all to read the article as I have merely touched on a few of the important points.

Spiritual spring cleaning.

Now *that* is an interesting term, to be sure.

There are many things that clutter us up spiritually, such as nagging anxieties, jealousy, anger, resentment, regret, fear, guilt, skepticism, cynicism, failure to be true to oneself, greed, the constant busyness that keeps us stuck in the quagmire of frustration.

Likewise for the reading of indoctrinational material, the watching of indoctrinational material, and the talking about indoctrinational material, all of which serve to keep us prisoner to negativity.

These are the issues that weigh us down with a heavy heart.

These are the issues that leave us feeling depressed, powerless and unbalanced.

These are the issues that block our energy, thereby hindering our spiritual growth.

Find a place of solitude, away from work, TV, cell phones and emails. In the silence, take the time to get in touch with all the inner rumblings, paying attention to what your inner teacher has to say.

Silence and stillness are healthy for the soul.

Meditation, a union of mind and body, is an adventure in self-discovery. In fact, scientists are now discovering that meditation has a biological effect on the body.

It has even been suggested, by means of a small-scale study, that meditation can boost parts of the brain as well as the immune system.

Paradigms are belief systems that we operate from. It is in getting to know the intricacies of your personal operating system that you come to know yourself in the now.

Meditation has been practiced since ancient times, but mainly in the East. As such, meditation can be used to ascertain and expand the paradigm from which you operate.

In essence, meditation leads to peace and tranquility, as well as equanimity of mind.

In keeping, equanimity of mind leads to self-realization or the super-conscious state of mind.

Do take the time to check out these related websites.

<u>Ananda Online: A Simple Meditation Technique</u> [77]

<u>Four Basic Elements to Traditional Meditation</u> [78]

<u>Free Meditations: How To Meditate and Attain Inner Peace and Freedom</u> [79]

<u>How To Meditate and Channel Awareness Inwards</u> [80]

<u>Introduction to Meditation</u> [81]

<u>Meditation Exercises and Techniques</u> [82]

---

[77] http://www.ananda.org/meditation/technique.html
[78] http://1stholistic.com/Meditation/hol_meditation_four_basic_elements.htm
[79] http://freemeditations.com
[80] http://www.lifepositive.com/meditation.html
[81] http://yogateacher.com/text/meditation/on-line/general.html
[82] http://www.abc-of-yoga.com/meditation/home.asp

The Ultimate Enlightenment For 2012

Meditation For Spiritual Awakening and Emotional Well-Being [83]

Meditation Techniques: Their Purpose and Benefits [84]

The Meditation Site [85]

The Physiology of Meditation [86]

You Are Your Path [87]

---

[83] http://www.yogajournal.com/meditation/564_1.cfm
[84] http://www.successconsciousness.com/index_000064.htm
[85] http://www.feedback.nildram.co.uk/richardebbs/meditation/meditationindex.htm
[86] http://ejmas.com/pt/ptart_shin_0400.htm
[87] http://www.youareyourpath.com

The Ultimate Enlightenment For 2012

Madonna in Bronze

Photo by Kevin Peuhkurinen

http://www.flickr.com/photos/wolfhound/241519863/

Reprinted herein with permission

Religious Affiliation Does Not Matter

Having worked through the VP exercises of the previous chapter, it is clear that one's religious affiliation is of no matter. Although, as a Gnostic seeker, religion is a form of spiritual control that I no longer subscribe to, it is still deemed important to many.

God, Goddess, the Great Spirit, the Universal Spirit, Buddha, whomever or whatever you emulate, exists within. The truth is that we have never been separated from our Creator, although this is what most have been led to believe, courtesy of organized religion.

In knowing that God resides within, there is no duality, there is no separation; hence, one's true spiritual awareness lies in making the connection that God exists within every being living on the planet.

If I may share some additional words from Nick Bunick.

The Ultimate Enlightenment For 2012

Nick has a vision of God being on top of a mountain with each and every one of us traversing that mountain, traveling up the road to reach the top and be at one with God. [88]

In continuation, the vehicle in which we are traveling in is our religious beliefs, our metaphysical beliefs, our value systems, how we conduct our way of life, and when we reach a certain height, as we get closer to the top of the mountain, we abandon the vehicle in which we are traveling, for we no longer want to be restricted to dogma and doctrine. [89]

Having finally reached the height of this great mountain, we find that our relationship with God is one that is truly spiritual, that we are all truly brothers and sisters, not only with our words and thoughts, but also in our deeds. [90]

All envision God in their manner of choice.

---

[88] Bunick, Nick. (1998). *In God's Truth* (p 73). Charlottesville, VA: Hampton Roads Publishing Company, Inc.
[89] Ibid.
[90] Ibid.

Although it is impossible for us, in our human form, to truly see God, "we can experience God in every moment of our lives, through everything that we can see, feel, hear and touch that is good, that brings us happiness, joy, serenity, peace, pleasure, and comfort" [91] for all are manifestations of the Creator.

Before incarnating on this earth plane, we existed in the spiritual dimension, a child of God created from God's spirit. We are all sparks of the Divine, part of the whole, part of the Creator.

In keeping with this train of thought, Nick further states that we are not a human being, that by coincidence, has a spirit and a soul; in respect, we are a spirit with a soul that is having a human experience. [92]

Hence, Spirit is everlasting, Spirit is immortal.

One's soul is the personality, the intellect, the memories.

One's soul changes with each and every human experience.

---

[91] Bunick, Nick. (1998). *In God's Truth* (p 73). Charlottesville, VA: Hampton Roads Publishing Company, Inc.
[92] Ibid, p 75.

Such is the relationship that exists between spirit and soul.

When each individual comes to understand "that there is no such thing as death, you come to understand God. When you come to understand there is no such thing as the monster Fear, you come to understand God. When you come to understand that God is our Father and Mother and that every one of us is a child of God, you come to understand God. When you come to understand that, if every one of us is a child of God, then we are all brothers and sisters, then you come to understand God." [93]

Mick continues in same vein, saying that "when you provide love and compassion to your brothers and sisters, you yourself, are manifesting God. When you come to understand that our bodies are nurtured by food and rest, but our spirits and souls are nurtured by experiencing love and compassion, then you come to understand and know God." [94]

God does not profess to have a formal religion.

---

[93] Bunick, Nick. (1998). *In God's Truth* (pp 76-77). Charlottesville, VA: Hampton Roads Publishing Company, Inc.
[94] Ibid, pp 77-78.

The Ultimate Enlightenment For 2012

I am of the belief, as is Nick, that God would embrace all religions that teach the same messages: love and compassion. This is why I continue to feel anger when religious preachers and teachers try to place a burden of guilt on their parishioners and students by preaching that we are responsible for the crucifixion of Jesus, an act which took place 2,000 years ago.

The greatest lie one could commit "is to commit a lie in the name of God. The greatest crime a person can commit is to commit a crime in the name of God. The greatest sin a person can commit is to commit a sin in the name of God." [95]

Throughout history, we have seen, and are, most unfortunately, continuing to see, many examples of such atrocities.

If you take the time to reflect back on the years 1097 to 1270, two hundred years of murder, rape, plunder and torture under the guise of religious righteousness, you only need ask yourself how many innocent lives were taken in the

---

[95] Bunick, Nick. (1998). *In God's Truth* (p 106). Charlottesville, VA: Hampton Roads Publishing Company, Inc.

name of the so-called Holy Crusades? Likewise for the gruesome Inquisition, that followed.

How about the German concentration camps of the second World War?

These lives were declared forfeit mainly because they adhered to a different religious belief from that of the mainstream.

Over the course of history, I believe that we have created and perceived God to be what our needs have dictated; as a result, this is what quickly led to power and control by a select few.

As we leave the earth plane, I, too, believe that "we will enter the level of the spiritual world consistent with how high we had climbed the mountain, consistent with the level of our spiritual attainment on earth." [96]

---

[96] Bunick, Nick. (1998). *In God's Truth* (p 147). Charlottesville, VA: Hampton Roads Publishing Company, Inc.

Such is in keeping with the fact that we are here to learn lessons based on karma, a Sanskrit word that means action and is based on both rewards and compensation of previous incarnational acts.

As so succinctly put by Nick, this "natural system of birth and death and rebirth continues until we reach the top of the mountain and do not have to come back on earth again, in a mortal body." [97]

Pythagoras, the Greek philosopher, "not only believed in reincarnation, but claimed that he received as a gift the memory of his soul's past lives." [98] Pythagoras died 500 years before Jesus was born.

Aristotle, as well as his teacher Plato for that matter, believed in reincarnation. He stated in a number of his writings "that the soul of man is immortal and can perform its proper functions by continuing to transmigrate into different physical bodies at different time." [99] Aristotle died 322 years before Jesus was born.

---

[97] Bunick, Nick. (1998). *In God's Truth* (p 150). Charlottesville, VA: Hampton Roads Publishing Company, Inc.
[98] Ibid.
[99] Ibid, p 151.

The great philosopher Plutarch died 120 years before Jesus was born. It was he who stated that "every soul was ordained to wander between incarnations in the spiritual world until driven down again to earth and coupled with human bodies." [100]

The Roman General, Julius Caesar, died 44 years before Jesus was born. In his words, "souls do not become extinct, but pass after death from one body to another." [101]

The Roman philosopher Cicero died 43 years before Jesus was born. It was he who stated that "there was strong proof of men knowing most things before birth, and, when they are children, they grasp enumerable facts with such speed as to show they are not then taking them in for the first time, but remember them and recall them from past lives." [102]

---

[100] Bunick, Nick. (1998). *In God's Truth* (p 151). Charlottesville, VA: Hampton Roads Publishing Company, Inc.
[101] Ibid.
[102] Ibid.

The Roman poet Virgil died 19 years before Jesus was born. He stated that "all souls, after they have passed away, are summoned by the divine ones again. In this way they become forgetful of their former earth life and revisit the world, willing to return again to new living bodies." [103]

Jesus was *also* a believer in reincarnation.

Likewise for a significant number of early church pillars such as St. Augustine, Clement of Alexandria, Justin Martyr, St. Gregory of Nyssa and St. Jerome, until the belief was banned by the early Roman Church in 553 AD.

Origen, the most prominent, most distinguished and most influential of the early church fathers, was a believer in reincarnation; unfortunately, he was deemed a heretic.

The tragedy, herein, is that "Christians have been led to believe that the doctrine of reincarnation has never been part of the Christian faith." [104]

---

[103] Bunick, Nick. (1998). *In God's Truth* (p 151). Charlottesville, VA: Hampton Roads Publishing Company, Inc.

[104] Walker III, Ethan. (2003). *The Mystic Christ: The Light of Non-Duality and the Path of Love According to the Life*

In essence, the doctrine of reincarnation was banished because it gave "power and authority to the people. Reincarnation contradicted the aspirations of a few bishops and deacons who felt they alone should dispense the truth to the multitudes. This authoritarian strangle-hold is strengthened by the doctrine of "one chance-one life" because a person who wrongly chose to think for him/herself, dismissing the authority of the hierarchy, would not get another chance to put things aright if s/he guessed wrongly." [105]

One has to ask what was offered in its place?

Are you ready for the answer?

The belief in "a punishing God; the belief in a supernatural evil force that is competing with God for your will and your mind; the belief that, if the devil succeeds, you will be condemned to live and be tortured for eternity in a place called hell; the belief that you should carry the guilt and responsibility on your shoulders that our beloved brother

---

and Teachings of Jesus (p 184). Norman, OK: Devi Press Inc.
[105] Walker III, Ethan. (2003). *The Mystic Christ: The Light of Non-Duality and the Path of Love According to the Life and Teachings of Jesus* (p 188). Norman, OK: Devi Press Inc.

died on the cross two thousand years ago because of your sins; the belief that you and your children are born in sin." [106]

Fear and guilt are creations of the medieval church that still exist to this day.

It takes considerable strength and courage to break free from these bonds, all in an effort to jump into the unknown depths of the inner search for truth.

I should know, given that it has taken me close to 30 years to rid myself of this unnecessary baggage.

Life is but a journey. You have a right to reject that which is not conducive to your learning to be at one with God.

It is in helping others that you show your love for God, that you nurture your own spirit and soul.

It is in helping others, that you also help yourself. You also become a manifestation of God. Who would have thought that it was so simple a task?

---

[106] Bunick, Nick. (1998). *In God's Truth* (p 166). Charlottesville, VA: Hampton Roads Publishing Company, Inc.

Love is the greatest manifestation of God one can give to another.

Love is the greatest manifestation of God one can receive from another.

It is imperative that you "learn how to express love to others. Let others feel your love by your words, your body language, your attitude, the look in your eyes, your behavior and your actions. Not only will you touch the lives of thousands of people, but you, yourself, will feel a greater joy and harmony inside of you than you have ever felt before." [107]

In keeping, it is of the utmost importance that we take the time to live more authentically, as per these six principles [108] identified by Robert Rabbin, until they help one become real.

---

[107] Bunick, Nick. (1998). *In God's Truth* (p 180). Charlottesville, VA: Hampton Roads Publishing Company, Inc.
[108] Rabbin, Robert. (2004). *Six Principles of Authentic Living*.
Retrieved November 17, 2004, from http://www.robertrabbin.com/reading-room/talks-and-interviews/a.php?article=sixprinciplesforauthenticliving

Such puts me in mind of the story *The Velveteen Rabbit* by Margery Williams.

Live your own life. It takes both strength and courage to live your own life as opposed to living the life that someone else wants, or expects, you to live.

Be persistent. Do not give up. Keep building your dream, whatever it may be. Be persistent, but also flexible. Flexibility allows us to learn from our mistakes, and to learn from others, embracing change when necessary.

Respect other people. Especially those that you do not like or who are so completely different from you that you appear to have no common ground. Respecting other people invites them to respect you. If you do no harm to others, and they, in turn, respond in kind, one can imagine the beauty of this planet.

Express gratitude and appreciation. To everyone, every single day. It takes but a moment, and yet it makes all the difference in the world. This is how we go about creating heaven on earth.

Live in the moment. Now is the only time there is. Make it count. Be your very best in this moment. Face your fears in this moment. Speak the truth of you in this moment. Live from the depths of your soul in this moment.

The Ultimate Enlightenment For 2012

Do not become cynical and selfish. We all face an uncertain future, but it is one that we face together. It may seem that we cannot change things, but we must continue to stand up for righteousness and justice for all. Take care of yourself and your families, but continue to make a contribution to others. Find a way to be of service to the world. Find a way to be of service to others. Keep a positive outlook. Be optimistic.

Paradigm Shift

What is a paradigm?

The word paradigm refers to a conceptual framework, a belief system, an overall perspective, through which we see and interpret the world. As such, one's paradigm determines what they are able to see, how they think and what they do. How one views the world, by way of a spiritual tradition, is part of the individual paradigm to which we adhere.

Paradigms are relative, subjective and personal.

While we *assume* that the way we see things is the way they really are, in truth, our paradigms become perceptible to us only when we encounter one that differs from our own.

You can begin to determine your own personal paradigm by reflecting on the following questions.

→ Do you see the world as a battlefield with good forces pitting against evil, an ancient tradition that goes back to the Zoroastrians, the Manichaeans, the Cathars?

→ Do you see the world as a classroom where you come to learn and are put through a multitude of tests?

The Ultimate Enlightenment For 2012

→ Do you see the world as a trap, where you attempt to disentangle yourselves in an attempt to ascend to a higher plane of tranquility?

→ Do you see the world as a collection of inanimate objects, merely to accumulate, thereby stroking the ego?

→ Do you see the world as a partner, attempting to commune more with nature in an effort to become more fully human?

→ Do you see the world as self, an interconnected whole with each playing an important role in the overall script of life?

→ What are your paradigms?

→ What set of structures or belief system do you operate from?

→ How are these paradigms serving you in this life?

One way to know yourself, or at least where you are now, is to get to know the intricacies of your operating system.

→ What do you value?

→ What are your needs?

The Ultimate Enlightenment For 2012

→ What are your feelings?

→ What matters to you?

→ How do you fit into the grand scheme called life?

→ How do you know what you know?

→ What is truth?

The more you know about who you are, the easier it is to respond (as opposed to react) to life.

Everything we do and say is the expression of our beliefs about the world.

Finding the underlying beliefs can lead to insights and understanding.

As one would expect, paradigms shift when we change from one way of thinking to another way of thinking.

It can be compared to a revolution, a transformation, a sort of metamorphosis, if you will; however, it is not simply something that just happens out of the blue and on its own; rather, it is driven by agents of change.

Accordingly, change is usually difficult.

How is it, then, that paradigms shift?

World views emerge to solve problems.

For an emerging new world view to take hold, the majority have to fully understand, aside from pure abstract intellect, that the current way of thinking is no longer adequate to solve the problems that are faced.

It is not enough to be passionate about the change that is needed, nor is it satisfactory to suppress the voices of those in disagreement.

We are currently being challenged to combine rational and non-rational (faith, intuition, spiritual insight, nature, body-based wisdom) ways of thinking.

As a result, a new world view is always in the process of arriving.

The Ultimate Enlightenment For 2012

Yeshua

Commissioned by Nick Bunick

Author of *In God's Truth*

Reprinted herein with permission

Transformation

Science is revealing that the earth's base resonant frequency is increasing and that the magnetic fields of the planet are dropping. Such is reflected in the shifting migration patterns of animals.

As we live and walk about the surface of our planet, the frequency of the soil is rising and affecting everything on the planet.

When soil frequency rises, many changes occur in people, animals and plants.

Without judgment, there is no better time for mental, physical and emotional patterns, conditioning, belief systems, attitudes, institutions, thought forms and programming to be dismantled.

With the frequencies of the planet rising at a considerable rate, that which we think or desire is becoming actualized.

In keeping, the same is also happening to our physical bodies; if you feel like you are being pulled in two directions, it is because you are.

The Ultimate Enlightenment For 2012

What is happening to Mother Earth is also happening to her children.

This means that old emotional, mental and spiritual baggage is being loosened, making it easier to let go of what is no longer useful.

You find that your resistance begins to drop.

You actually begin to wonder why certain people, places and situations were so important to you in the first place.

Undoubtedly, this change may feel quite chaotic at times, given that things are moving quickly.

We walk about in matter-energy bodies that carry a certain density. In connection with both the rising vibrational frequency and the lowering of magnetic fields, our physical bodies are being transmuted into more refined, less dense, light bodies.

Interaction and exchange is taking place on a level of higher consciousness.

We are reconnecting our minds to the shared universal consciousness, both with each other and with beings who may live in another dimension or level of reality.

The Ultimate Enlightenment For 2012

Our bodies are being activated and altered by this change; as a result, transformation is taking place.

Our DNA holds an ancient blueprint for the budding and flowering of the radiant Christ consciousness to step forth.

This is what we have been praying for, asking for, invoking through conscious meditation and activation.

In essence, we are becoming a new species of the Light, a new vibrational being; having done so, we will never be the same.

In passing from one molecular density to a new molecular density of a higher vibrational level, we are transforming.

We are becoming more of our Divine selves.

Our biological rhythms are altering. The magnetic fields of the brain are working with more light. The brain frequency is being raised; some people call it going into Zero Point where there is no resistance.

In the dropping of resistance, in the dropping of density, we are discovering that the old programs no longer work. This is where we will truly experience the meaning of *Let Go and Let God*.

As energy and matter are changing, certain parts of the body may feel stronger at times than others. All the grids of the body are realigning. As this biological rearrangement is taking place, you are going to feel it.

You may feel very tired, and sometimes it will come on suddenly. Take the time to rest.

There may also be a type of detoxification taking place, resulting in flu-like symptoms, discomfort, aches, and a fever that, while fever-like, is not really fever.

There may be times where you feel dizzy and out of control, but then it goes away.

You may also feel somewhat clumsy, walking into walls and bumping into things.

Some changes are occurring with eyesight and hearing, so you may feel pain in the eyes and ears. Being able to see between worlds may be experienced.

Our physical brains are altering. You may experience discomfort in the third eye and crown chakra areas because the pineal gland is coming back into alignment with its divine nature.

The Ultimate Enlightenment For 2012

We need to feel compassion for humanity, for ourselves, as we are going through this shift, a conscious metamorphosis and a conscious ascension.

During this time, we can only imagine what the full activation of our DNA will allow us to accomplish and manifest for Planetary healing and restoration.

You may find the following websites to be of additional assistance.

About Our New Chakras [109]

DNA Upgrades: Making The New You [110]

Foundation For A New Consciousness [111]

Principles of Personal Transformation [112]

Shifting Paradigms of Consciousness [113]

---

[109] http://www.wistancia.com/onc.htm
[110] http://www.2012.com.au/DNA_upgrades.html
[111] http://www.westgatehouse.com/fchap1.html
[112] http://www.weboflove.org/wingmakers
[113] http://www.weboflove.org/consciousnessparadigms

The Ultimate Enlightenment For 2012

What On Earth Is Happening To Our Bodies? [114]

---

[114] http://www.wistancia.com/articles/WoE-Bodies.htm

The Ultimate Enlightenment For 2012

Peaceful Buddha

Unplugging From The Matrix

Is truth worth pursuing? Is reality worth pursuing? These are very heady questions and yet they become the ultimate in deciding whether or not to unplug from The Matrix.

If we take the blue pill, we will remain where we are, as we have always been, "in a life consisting of habit, of things we believe we know." [115]

---

[115] Droar, Dave. *Matrix Philosophy - Blue or Red Pill?* Retrieved December 24, 2006, from http://www.arrod.co.uk/essays/matrix.php

The Ultimate Enlightenment For 2012

This is where one is comfortable, "not needing the truth to live." [116]

The red pill, on the other hand, is an unknown; we are told "that it can help us find the truth and yet we do not know what that truth is." [117]

In essence, "the red pill symbolizes risk, doubt and questioning," thereby leading one to "gamble their whole life and world on a reality they have never experienced." [118]

It is Morpheus who says to Neo ... *You have to understand that many people are not ready to be unplugged, and many of them are so inured, so hopelessly dependent on the system, that they will fight to protect it.*

---

[116] Droar, Dave. *Matrix Philosophy - Blue or Red Pill?* Retrieved December 24, 2006, from http://www.arrod.co.uk/essays/matrix.php
[117] Ibid.
[118] Ibid.

Why is it that "children ask a seemingly never-ending stream of questions from an early age" whereas "it is only with education and socialization that some people stop asking the questions?" [119]

It is the very act of asking these pertinent questions about truth and reality that become the starting point towards metamorphosis and enlightenment.

According to Droar, if one is "philosophically driven to seek the truth, then the act of questioning whether to seek it is, in itself, seeking the truth. As conscious minds we will always seek the truth." [120]

In keeping with truth, it is hoped that the reader will take the time to investigate these pertinent websites.

Escaping the Matrix Part 1 – Introduction [121]

---

[119] Droar, Dave. *Matrix Philosophy - Blue or Red Pill?* Retrieved December 24, 2006, from http://www.arrod.co.uk/essays/matrix.php
[120] Ibid.
[121] http://www.rumormillnews.com/cgi-bin/archive.cgi/read/84030

The Ultimate Enlightenment For 2012

Escaping the Matrix Part 2 – What Is The Matrix? [122]

Escaping the Matrix Part 3 – The NWO Paradox [123]

Escaping the Matrix Part 4 – Measuring Consciousness [124]

Escaping the Matrix Part 5 – Building Frequency 1 [125]

Escaping the Matrix Part 6 – Revelations and Disclosures, Section 1 [126]

Escaping the Matrix Part 6 – Revelations and Disclosures, Section 2 [127]

Escaping the Matrix Part 7 – Building Frequency 2 [128]

---

[122] http://www.rumormillnews.com/cgi-bin/archive.cgi/read/84054
[123] http://www.rumormillnews.com/cgi-bin/archive.cgi/read/84084
[124] http://www.rumormillnews.com/cgi-bin/archive.cgi/read/84145
[125] http://www.rumormillnews.com/cgi-bin/archive.cgi/read/84165
[126] http://www.rumormillnews.com/cgi-bin/archive.cgi/read/84327
[127] http://www.rumormillnews.com/cgi-bin/archive.cgi/read/84346

The Ultimate Enlightenment For 2012

Escaping the Matrix Part 8 – Living Environment [129]

Escaping the Matrix Part 9 – Personal Sovereignty [130]

Where To Now 1 – Programming The Shift [131]

Where To Now 2 – Seeking The Higher Path [132]

Where To Now 3 – Defining The New Path [133]

Where To Now 4 – The Cathar Prophecy [134]

Where To Now 5 – The Higher Principle [135]

---

[128] http://www.rumormillnews.com/cgi-bin/archive.cgi/read/84437
[129] http://www.rumormillnews.com/cgi-bin/archive.cgi/read/84513
[130] http://www.rumormillnews.com/cgi-bin/archive.cgi/read/85134
[131] http://www.rumormillnews.com/cgi-bin/archive.cgi/read/87081
[132] http://www.rumormillnews.com/cgi-bin/archive.cgi/read/87112
[133] http://www.rumormillnews.com/cgi-bin/archive.cgi/read/87186
[134] http://www.rumormillnews.com/cgi-bin/archive.cgi/read/87222
[135] http://www.rumormillnews.com/cgi-bin/archive.cgi/read/87245

Where To Now 6 – Steps, Part 1 [136]

Where To Now 7 – Steps, Part 2 [137]

Are You Living In A Computer Simulation? [138]

Interview with Sophia Stewart, Mother of the Matrix and The Terminator (January 9, 2005) [139]

Is The Matrix Gnostic or Christian? Part 1 [140]

Is The Matrix Gnostic or Christian? Part 2 [141]

Journal of Religion and Film – Buddhism, Christianity and The Matrix [142]

---

[136] http://www.rumormillnews.com/cgi-bin/archive.cgi/read/87384
[137] http://www.rumormillnews.com/cgi-bin/archive.cgi/read/87385
[138] http://www.simulation-argument.com
[139] http://playahata.com/pages/interviews/interview_sophiastewartpt1.htm
[140] http://www.decentfilms.com/sections/articles/2554
[141] http://www.decentfilms.com/sections/articles/matrixsequels.html
[142] http://www.unomaha.edu/jrf/thematrix.htm

The Ultimate Enlightenment For 2012

Journal of Religion and Film – Wake Up! Gnosticism and Buddhism in The Matrix [143]

The Divine Oracle: Sophia Stewart [144]

The Last Free City Forum: Discuss The Trilogy and The Animatrix Here [145]

The Matrix 101: Understanding The Matrix Trilogy [146]

The Matrix and Quantum Consciousness [147]

The Matrix Community [148]

The Matrix Essays Blog [149]

The Matrix Essays Collection [150]

The Matrix – Wikipedia [151]

---

[143] http://www.unomaha.edu/jrf/gnostic.htm
[144] http://wwwthedivineoraclesophia.blogspot.com/
[145] http://forums.thelastfreecity.com
[146] http://www.thematrix101.com
[147] http://www.tony5m17h.net/Matrix.html
[148] http://www.matrixcommunity.org
[149] http://matrixessays.blogspot.com
[150] http://www.wylfing.net/essays
[151] http://en.wikipedia.org/wiki/The_Matrix

The Ultimate Enlightenment For 2012

The New Gnostic Gospel [152]

The Philosophy of The Matrix: The Neurophilosopher's Weblog on The Molecular and Cellular Basis of Mind [153]

The Real Matrix, Part 1 (Steven Yates) [154]

The Real Matrix, Part 2 (Steven Yates) [155]

The Real Matrix, Part 3 (Steven Yates) [156]

The Real Matrix, Part 4 (Steven Yates) [157]

The Real Matrix, Part 5 (Steven Yates) [158]

The Real Matrix, Part 6 (Steven Yates) [159]

---

[152] http://www.envoymagazine.com/backissues/4.5/coverstory.html
[153] http://neurophilosophy.wordpress.com/2006/12/11/the-philosophy-of-the-matrix/
[154] http://www.newswithviews.com/Yates/steven.htm
[155] http://www.newswithviews.com/Yates/steven1.htm
[156] http://www.newswithviews.com/Yates/steven2.htm
[157] http://www.newswithviews.com/Yates/steven3.htm
[158] http://www.newswithviews.com/Yates/steven4.htm
[159] http://www.newswithviews.com/Yates/steven5.htm

The Ultimate Enlightenment For 2012

The Real Matrix, Part 7 (Steven Yates) [160]

The Simulation Argument: Why The Probability That You Are Living In A Matrix Is Quite High [161]

The Spiritual Message of The Matrix [162]

There Is No Spoon: The Matrix [163]

---

[160] http://www.newswithviews.com/Yates/steven6.htm
[161] http://www.simulation-argument.com/matrix.html
[162] http://www.npr.org/templates/story/story.php?storyId=1264976
[163] http://www.friesian.com/matrix.htm

Utopia Exists

Something that is very important is being in harmony with, one with, and a servant of, God. The primary key to that is loving unselfishly.

Once again, think about what you know of the lives of Buddha and Jesus. Do you see anything that conflicts or do you see examples of love and compassion, indications of similarity?

In terms of the paths that they spawned, the source of their teachings, the source of their examples, is it not the same understanding; is it not the same God?

They both teach of a oneness, or a oneness God, although they may disagree over names and/or particulars.

Most importantly, they believe in goodness, compassion and unselfish love as the way of life.

If I may draw an important conclusion from Jon Peniel, author of *The Children of the Law of One and The Lost Teachings of Atlantis*, in the words that follow.

The Ultimate Enlightenment For 2012

As we begin to expand our consciousness outside of ourselves, one begins to come to the realization that there is more to life, that there is more to the universe, than meets the physical eye. As we continue to grow in this spiritual consciousness, we understand the underlying connection: quite simply, that we are part of each other, that we are all one, brothers and sisters, all children of one universal God.

It becomes the discovering, experiencing and then practicing this unity that leads to "the beginning of the end of human mental and emotional suffering." [164]

It is in this spiritual consciousness mode that we both feel, and manifest, unselfish love by means of caring, kindness, compassion, giving and harmlessness, the earmarks of true spirituality as shared by Peniel.

Spirituality is simple.

Love is simple.

Truth is simple.

Enlightenment is simple.

---

[164] Walker III, Ethan. (2003). *The Mystic Christ: The Light of Non-Duality and the Path of Love According to the Life and Teachings of Jesus* (p 5). Norman, OK: Devi Press Inc.

The Ultimate Enlightenment For 2012

How is this so?

Simply by way of the re-kindling of a very old idea that requires many people to wake up and recognize the vital importance of the Golden Rule, while also working to apply it in their everyday lives.

The Golden Rule (which equates to being unselfishly loving) is so basic and simple that it has often been overlooked, and yet it is the most important spiritual teaching in the world.

At the core of the ancient teachings, in accordance with Peniel, it is the very crux of true spirituality for all people regardless of belief systems ... treating others as you would like to be treated.

Kindness, compassion, caring, giving and harmlessness, the virtues of unselfish love, the things that really matter, are the ultimate keys of returning to, and being in harmony with, the universal spirit.

Separateness gives most people of the world the basis for their belief in the illusion that we are separate beings, as opposed to one being manifesting itself in many forms. Peniel claims that it is this very separateness belief that has spawned differences (that I personally deem to have been unnecessary) as well as considerable selfishness.

The Ultimate Enlightenment For 2012

Any individual who wants to grow, attain enlightenment, or be a really good person, must completely re-evaluate their beliefs in the light of the effects those beliefs have, where they come from, and why. Who you are, and what you do, with universal consciousness, is key. This is why when you finally realize universal consciousness (when it finally is what you have achieved) it is called *enlightenment* or *illumination*. It is as if a light switch has been turned on in a life that has been lived in darkness.

In both Hinduism and Buddhism, the resurrection is referred to "as enlightenment or liberation. It is a dramatic change in one's life and one's perspective. It is the unshakable realization that we are not the body," [165] but that we are spirit, created from the very breath and image of the Creator, that we are the I AM.

Universal consciousness is attained when a person has a lasting experience in which they see through the illusion of separateness, thereby losing separate self consciousness; their consciousness then merges with the universe, thus they experience being one with the universe.

---

[165] Walker III, Ethan. (2003). *The Mystic Christ: The Light of Non-Duality and the Path of Love According to the Life and Teachings of Jesus* (p. 192). Norman, OK: Devi Press Inc.

The Ultimate Enlightenment For 2012

This may be the result of going through a consciousness psychological death experience, brought on by meditation and other aspects of a spiritual path.

The illusion of separateness dissolves in the awareness of oneness.

With the dissolution of the illusion of separateness, the separate self seems to die and a *rebirth* occurs. In keeping, separate self consciousness is transcended and transformed.

The dominant consciousness becomes that of the inner self, the part of us that is universal spirit, thus we have universal consciousness.

When experienced properly, a person is never the same.

When experienced properly, a person never sees things the same way again.

From then on, all things are understood in the light of the biggest picture, in the light of being one with the universal spirit (God) and selfishness becomes a thing of the past.

If you had an awareness of being one with everything, even God, how would you see things then?

How would you treat everyone?

The Ultimate Enlightenment For 2012

If you *absolutely knew* that every person you were dealing with is you, just in a different form, how would you treat yourself (others)?

Is there any point in stealing from yourself?

Is there any point in hurting yourself?

Is there any point in being tyrannical with yourself?

A being with universal consciousness loves everyone unselfishly, and is (within the needs of universal flow) giving, kind and compassionate.

It is as natural for a person with universal consciousness to be totally giving, as it is for a person with separate self consciousness to be selfish.

A person with universal consciousness is focused outward, akin to an energy beacon, a Sun, always giving energy.

In conclusion, piercing this illusion and attaining universal consciousness is the answer to all of the current problems of this world.

The closer you get to attaining universal consciousness, the greater your point of view will become and the more you will intuitively see the whole picture, or whole situation.

But while a person who has attained universal consciousness may see the whole picture to the greatest extent possible, even they may be unable to see it in its complete entirety while still embodied in the physical; such can, however, be achieved in deep meditation.

Upon returning to the physical following meditation, we can only grasp the essence of what we understood while in our ultimate point of view state; this is why getting out of our own way, allowing ourselves to be an instrument of the universal spirit (God), is the greatest wisdom that exists.

Know your true self and you will know the true story; know your whole self and you will know the wholeness of the truth. This is merely the modern equivalent to *know thyself* as per the Greek Philosopher, Socrates.

Virtually everyone will agree that kindness, compassion, caring and giving are good things. Taking it one step further, these spiritual values are far more significant than any belief, teaching, wisdom or knowledge that may be imparted.

All are the natural result of true spiritual growth.

Quite simply, if these qualities are not the outcome of your growth, then the growth is not really spiritual.

The Ultimate Enlightenment For 2012

True spiritual growth moves you away from the world of separateness and selfishness, toward universal consciousness and oneness.

Such a shift in consciousness can only result in caring for all, for you quickly realize that all beings are you (the universal spirit).

In every moment, we have the opportunity to contract or expand our awareness. Whilst there "are many paths to the top of the mountain," as per Michael Gelb, "there is only one summit – love." [166]

Clearly, love is the genetic code of the universe. To see God everywhere and in everyone "is the goal of our human existence. Everyone, without exception, is our brother and sister. This divine kinship also extends to mountains, rivers, plants, suns and universes. Everything is alive with God's infinite consciousness." [167]

---

[166] Gelb, Michael. (2004). *Da Vinci Decoded: Discovering the Spiritual Principles of Leonardo's Seven Principles* (p xx). New York, NY: Delacorte Press.

[167] Walker III, Ethan. (2003). *The Mystic Christ: The Light of Non-Duality and the Path of Love According to the Life and Teachings of Jesus* (p 8). Norman, OK: Devi Press Inc.

Time To Wake Up

As Neale Donald Walsch shared in an email dated April 14, 2006 ......

Why are we here, anyway? On the earth, I mean.

I believe there is a Process in place that is playing itself out, and in which we are playing a part – most of us without even knowing it.

The fascinating thing about this Process is that we don't have to know that we are playing a part in it in order to play a part in it. So the part that most of us are playing is being played unconsciously.

If I'm right about this, and by the way, most ancient mystics and modern-day spiritual teachers agree with my observation, then the idea here would be to become conscious. That is, to WAKE UP.

Yet, how does one do that?

Let this be our question for the day.

The Ultimate Enlightenment For 2012

Well, it's no fair asking a question without proposing an answer. So here is the answer I propose: We wake up by waking each OTHER up.

So that's our opportunity, that's our invitation.

We're invited to wake each other up on this planet, to let each other know that we are not all crazy, that nothing is really as it seems, that we have "fallen down the rabbit hole" and are seeing things through a glass darkly, and that if we but say the magic words we can live within this illusionary world in a way that can actually begin to make sense, that can bring us joy once again, that can end the largest amount of human suffering, and that can allow us to label as a "success" this human experiment.

The magic words we are invited to invoke are these ......

[1] **Nothing I see is real.**

[2] **The world is the world of my imagining.**

[3] **If I wish to change it, all I have to do is change my thought about it.**

[4] **From my thought about the world springs all of my reality.**

Then we have to get OTHERS to say the magic words as well. Ah ... that's the real trick. How do we get OTHERS to understand that we are all creating this present reality together and that it doesn't have to be this way?

How do we get OTHERS to understand that the killing and the fighting are not necessary? That there is ENOUGH. There's enough food, there's enough clothing, there's enough shelter, there's enough energy, there's enough opportunity, there's enough of all we need to be truly happy. There's enough for everybody. All we have to do is share.

What stops us from sharing? Ironically, the idea that there is "not enough." The fear that we are somehow going to "run out" of what we need. If we "run out," then what will we do?

And so, it's all about survival. We think that we need what we need in order to survive, and since there is "not enough" of what we need, we have to do two things:

[1] PROTECT the stuff we have, and [2] Get MORE

If we thought there was ENOUGH of all that we need to survive and be happy, all of our competitions, all of our conflicts, all of our stress and worry and concern and guarding the gate could end.

The Ultimate Enlightenment For 2012

I have come here today to bring you the Good News: THERE'S ENOUGH.

Those two simple words are all we need to change our realities. Will we embrace them? Can we believe them? Our lives – and the behaviors OF our lives – will be our answer to those questions.

We Are Our Own Future

We are on the verge of a reconciliation, a healing, of great significance between two polarities; a sacred marriage, if you will, between the long-dominant masculine, power seeking patriarchy (of the past 2,000 years) and the long-suppressed, but now ascending, nature-affirming, goddess worshiping feminine.

If we strip away "the sexual politics of our time and contemplate the eternal nature of the human psyche, we can easily see how complimentary these two fundamental modes of consciousness are. The masculine mode, sometimes associated with the left hemisphere of the cerebral cortex, is more analytical, focused and convergent; it is the mode for influencing the environment, for getting things done, for "doing". The feminine mode, sometimes associated with the right hemisphere, is more receptive, intuitive and divergent. This is the mode for sensitivity to the environment, for letting things be, for "being". Obviously, to be whole, we must integrate the masculine and feminine principles." [168]

Eileen Nauman believes, as do I, that "we choose a 'map' in which we live our lives in order to educate ourselves, pay back others (karma), receive Grace (Dharma) and develop continued strength and endurance" [169] on our way back to God, Great Spirit, or whomever you believe in.

What we are doing to others, we are doing to ourselves; in keeping, what we do to ourselves, plays out to others as well.

The key is that no matter what you are going through, you must be aware of others, be kind, be thoughtful, be there as much as you can for others.

---

[168] Gelb, Michael. (2004). *Da Vinci Decoded: Discovering the Spiritual Principles of Leonardo's Seven Principles* (p 8). New York, NY: Delacorte Press.
[169] Nauman, Eileen. (2006). *Preparing for the Global Shift - Moving to the LIGHT from the DARK: How to Do It.* Retrieved July 13, 2006, from http://www.medicinegarden.com/metaphysics/globalshift2006.html and can be reached at docbones@gotsky.com

Genuine love is akin to "the sun that shines on all people regardless of what they have done. It simply shines for its own sake and expects nothing in return. A person who can step into pure love has arrived at the kingdom of God." [170]

If we go away from love "by allowing anger and hatred to control our lives, then we go away from Heaven, and we unwittingly become bedfellows with hell. If we destroy love, our lives will become hell as certainly as darkness must fall when the sun disappears from the sky. Love is the liberator. Love is the flow of life itself. Love is the destroyer of ignorance, for the ego cannot survive in the presence of pure love. It takes courage to surrender to love because it means the death of the ego." [171]

The ultimate key to individual creativity and fulfillment lies in the integration of male (yin) and female (yang).

The Grail, which all seek, merely represents the fulfillment of the highest spiritual potentialities of the human consciousness.

---

[170] Walker III, Ethan. (2003). *The Mystic Christ: The Light of Non-Duality and the Path of Love According to the Life and Teachings of Jesus* (p 233). Norman, OK: Devi Press Inc.

[171] Ibid.

In other words, the treasure, the Grail, resides within. It is the quest itself, and what it tells us about ourselves, that is of significant importance.

As so beautifully penned by my Aussie friend, Brian McFarlane, and shared with me in an email dated June 14, 2007, with permission to include herein.

Love is the Holy Grail,

It is truly God defined.

Truth is the Philosopher's Stone,

It is truly God revealed.

When the Stone and Grail are found,

Justice and Mercy kiss.

The second coming of Christ is merely "the recognition of Christ as the living presence at the center of one's own being and has nothing to do with the physical body of Jesus making another appearance." [172]

---

[172] Walker III, Ethan. (2003). *The Mystic Christ: The Light of Non-Duality and the Path of Love According to the Life*

Instead, it is an affair of the heart.

When the ego has been transcended, "love flows unimpeded from the center of our being as a wellspring, a river of divine grace. This manifests outwardly as pure selfless love for all beings. Compassion is love in action." [173]

Love is the true guiding light; one who has found pure selfless love has found God.

True happiness is found in what we give, not in what we take.

In essence, we are who we have been waiting for.

Additional websites to browse as you continue your inner search.

<u>Fire The Grid: We Can Help Save The Earth</u> [174]

---

and Teachings of Jesus (p 203). Norman, OK: Devi Press Inc.
[173] Walker III, Ethan. (2003). *The Mystic Christ: The Light of Non-Duality and the Path of Love According to the Life and Teachings of Jesus* (p 232). Norman, OK: Devi Press Inc.
[174] http://www.firethegrid.com/eng/home-fr-eng.htm

The Ultimate Enlightenment For 2012

Joseph Campbell Foundation [175]

Medicine Garden (Eileen Nauman) [176]

Parallels Between The Hopi and The Sumerian Culture [177]

Unity

---

[175] http://jcf.org/
[176] http://www.medicinegarden.com/
[177] http://www.dreamscape.com/morgana/parallel.htm

Quotable "The Secret" Quotes

I am available to more good than I have ever imagined, experienced or realized before.

~ Reverend Dr. Michael Beckwith ~

I choose, today, to give myself the best life ever.

~ Lisa Nichols ~

Nothing new can come into your life unless you open yourself up to being grateful for what you already have.

~ Reverend Dr. Michael Beckwith ~

Spiritual growth is about allowing that which is unconscious to become conscious.

~ Reverend Dr. Michael Beckwith ~

The Ultimate Enlightenment For 2012

As we become more awake, more aware, our life is filled with that kind of vibration, love, peace joy, wisdom, harmony, that kind of feeling tone. To grow spiritually is actually to become more aware of who you really are.

~ Reverend Dr. Michael Beckwith ~

True forgiveness is when you can say the following to the person who hurt you ... "Thank you for giving me that experience".

~ James Arthur Ray ~

Here's what I encourage people to ask themselves, how does this serve me? If you're really willing to dig, there's a lesson in there. And, secondly, what can I learn from this situation?

~ James Arthur Ray ~

The Ultimate Enlightenment For 2012

I am the first example of how the world is supposed to love me. We expect someone to show us our greatness when [instead] *I am supposed to show up understanding my greatness and allowing you to celebrate it with me.*

~ Lisa Nichols ~

We've Been Living In A Dream World

Oscar Wilde once re-marked ... *Most people are other people; their thoughts are someone else's opinions, their lives a mimicry, their passions a quotation.*

As he so wryly observed, the vast majority of us are not who we've been pretending to be, and the lives we've been living until now are molded according to rules and values that are not our own.

Most of humanity is stuck in someone else's discarded chewing gum and has yet to break free.

Unless you have been brave enough to forsake this trap, here is your likely portrait ......

→ your religious convictions are those of your parents or community

→ you root for your hometown sports teams

→ your political allegiances conform to the party system that society offers

The Ultimate Enlightenment For 2012

→ you are an avid observer of the cultural pageantry, like the Super Bowl and the Oscars

→ your holidays are the standard ones, such as Christmas, New Year's Eve and Independence Day

→ you look to your political and religious leaders for guidance and protection

→ you feel driven to succeed: to make more money, to live a better life

These are worthy and desirable choices that hold families and societies together.

They make you who you are, you might argue. True, but only if you are content with admiring the wrapping and never looking inside the box.

If you dared to look, you'd discover how these basic thoughts originate in a fundamental belief formed during the first years of your life – that survival depends on obeying the rules.

Children typically bend their perceptions and interpretations of reality to match those of their parents and others who care for them. They find clever ways to please in order to receive attention and belong.

The Ultimate Enlightenment For 2012

As they grow up, the people and issues may change over time, but the initial patterns of conformity remain deeply ingrained in the subconscious.

The price for surrendering to consensus is steep. It is nothing less than the loss of individuality and curiosity.

Without these two magnificent attributes, you disengage from the grandness of the creation and implode into the holographic illusion humans have come to call reality.

You become one of Oscar Wilde's other people, thinking someone else's opinions and assuming they are your own.

We are trapped in the daily drama the culture and media feed us (mortgages, sporting events, tsunamis, sex offenders, AIDS, terrorism, global warming, corrupt governments and economic inequities), all demanding our attention.

The matrix plays us like an instrument. A thirty-second news bite can push your buttons.

We get hooked and riled, liberally lacing our collective guts with corrosive bio-chemicals unleashed by our righteous indignation.

This condition is virtually universal.

The Ultimate Enlightenment For 2012

It is also the underlying cause of the world as we know it.

People cling so tightly to their personal and social identities that they are blinded to anything that does not validate them. The inevitable product is a world of war, greed, and competition, driven by paranoia and fear.

The way out is easier than anyone might imagine; however, very few summon the courage, for it requires them to leave the comfort of their known world and walk alone, unaided by the crutch of belief and dogma, into the domain of pure consciousness.

Most people would rather get caught up in the business of earning a living, raising a family, or helping their community, than deal with the unsettling immensity of All That Is.

Yet it seems that all humans are meant to take this epic journey of discovery at some point in their series of lives on this planet.

If you choose to walk this path, you will find yourself gaining a new perspective – that of consciousness, where the mind, with its judgments and emotions, ceases to dominate and the heart is your only reliable guide.

The Ultimate Enlightenment For 2012

The great issues of your daily life that once demanded your attention now seem wondrously arbitrary and irrelevant, simply interesting experiences that lasted far too long and became unnecessarily weighty.

You now see the illusion for what it is: a game-board projection designed so aspects of the Oneness can experience duality, fear, and separation. It is no more real than a programmed matrix in a computer game.

You and I are merely units of awareness projected into the matrix, defining ourselves by the points through which we view and believe what we see to be reality.

Who did the projecting?

You.

Who is the projection?

There is only you.

How do you get to this liberating place from which you can see the larger picture?

The cosmic formula of creation is gloriously simple.

Attention + Intention = Manifestation

Nothing in the universe evades this law. The reality you perceive is entirely a function of the only two forces at your command: your attention and your intention.

Bring conscious awareness to this equation, consciously monitor your attention and intention and what you are manifesting, and everything changes.

Through this ongoing process of self-observation it will become increasingly clear that the part of you that is projected into the illusion is in trouble. This realization in fact marks the beginning of your journey out of the illusion.

Once you begin to couple the law of $A + I = M$ with the concept of Oneness, you begin to see a completely different picture.

You are All That Is.

There is nowhere for you to go, nothing to attain, no lessons to learn.

If you buy into the reality that you are an earthbound human stuck in the struggle of life, presto, there you are.

If you focus on the part of you that is watching you flounder in the illusion, snap, you're free. It can't get much easier than that.

The Ultimate Enlightenment For 2012

Yet why are so few of us awake? The written or spoken word can do no more than point the way. And trading one belief system for another accomplishes nothing.

The answer lies elsewhere. Waking up is a consequence of induction.

Just a few years ago you might have placed yourself in the presence of a guru or master and, through devotion, discipline, or some other practice, gradually assumed some of his or her enlightenment.

Now using the law of $A + I = M$, you become your own master.

By focusing your attention on the part of you that is watching the rest of you floundering in the illusion, you are taking a giant step in restoring control over how your attention is commanded.

If you add the intention of reclaiming your essence, you complete the formula that can only result in the manifestation of whatever your curiosity seeks to explore.

The payoff of having been so deeply mired in the illusion that you nearly succumbed is compassion for those still stuck in the matrix, coupled with a large dose of humility.

The Ultimate Enlightenment For 2012

You have learned that the illusion is perfect exactly as it is.

The only thing that needs to change is the point from which we view it.

Now all that's left is for you to summon the courage to begin the journey home.

Jean-Claude Koven is a writer and speaker based in Rancho Mirage, CA. He is the author of <u>Going Deeper: How To Make Sense of Your Life When Your Life Makes No Sense</u>, the Allbook's Reviews editor's choice for the best metaphysical book of 2004.

He was also the recipient of USABookNews.com best metaphysical book award. For more information, please visit http://www.prismhouse.com/

Copyright © 2005

Jean-Claude Koven – All Rights Reserved

This article is copyrighted but you have permission to share it through any medium as long as the proper copyright and credit line is included.

Peace Really Does Depend On You

The solution for worldwide peace has always been there, right under our noses, but it often requires more of us than we seem willing to give. Now, with our backs to the wall, we have run out of options. The choice is simple: act or perish.

Ever since the outbreak of hostilities between the Israeli Defense Forces (IDF) and Hezbollah, my email inbox has been jammed with requests to send prayers, light candles, link up with meditation groups, sign petitions, send light and love, and a host of similar calls to inaction. The latest one, forwarded by a friend, sported the subject line: "Help Stop the Bloodshed in the Middle East."

The email requested that I join in signing a petition "calling on US President Bush, UK Prime Minister Blair, and Israeli Prime Minister Olmert to support Kofi Annan's proposal. If millions of people join this call, and we advertise our views in newspapers in the US, UK, and Israel, we can help pressure these leaders to stop the fighting."

A link was provided to the Stop the Bloodshed: Ceasefire Now website: http://www.ceasefirecampaign.org/

The Ultimate Enlightenment For 2012

The organizer of the website wants at least 100,000 signatures on their petition. There is little doubt that they will achieve it.

My friend had added her sentiments to the email before forwarding it to her distribution list: "I'm sending this on because I believe it to be a good way of demonstrating that we are many millions who don't believe in the 'eye for an eye' reaction which only leads to never-ending violence and grief. And the UN really needs a show of support!"

Her email remained in my inbox for several days as I struggled with how I wanted to respond. How easy it would have been to add my name to the growing list of supporters, believing/pretending that I was making a contribution to peace in our time.

Anyone who reads my articles knows that the present conflict concerns me greatly. In fact, I have been spending quite a bit of time lately digging into the story behind the story.

What I have found is deeply disturbing – nothing is what the combatants, the media, and the debating nations would have us believe.

Go to http://prismhouse.com/upiforum/123.php

The Ultimate Enlightenment For 2012

Supporting the UN in this matter is like attempting to stop a rape by sending a donation to the Society for the Reformation of Manners.

In fact, our language and culture have completely lost touch with the meaning of the word "peace." As with so many things in this dualistic illusion we live in, the term has both a negative and a positive aspect.

The difference between them is not at all trivial; indeed, it lies at the heart of both the problem currently manifesting in the Middle East and its solution.

The negative connotation of peace only expresses the absence of its perceived opposite. From this perspective, peace is what fills the spaces between hostilities; in other words, peace has no distinct properties of its own, it is merely the absence of war.

The positive meaning of peace, on the other hand, refers to a palpable internal quality arising out of love, aesthetics, spiritual practice, and a host of other activities that touch and personally transform us as individuals.

It is not the peace between (which implies separation) but the peace within (which speaks of unity) that we should be seeking.

The Ultimate Enlightenment For 2012

It is a travesty of our language and culture that the same word is so loosely applied to both conditions; because of it, otherwise caring and intelligent people turn too easily into sloppy thinkers.

Negative peace is an inadequate, Band-Aid response to a gushing artery. Positive peace is the only answer, but it does not come as easily as adding one's name to a petition, wearing wrist bands, or joining prayer circles suggests.

Creating positive peace is not the business of groups or negotiations; it is not achieved through organizations, nations, religions, or, heaven help me, well intentioned emails.

Positive peace is an exquisite pearl that forms initially in response to the irritation of the world's condition, and then is perfected over the years by sustained personal effort.

I have come to realize that when I go to sleep at night believing something and wake up the next morning believing the same thing, it's no big deal. It merely means that I'm stuck and need to shift.

Anyone following world events over the past few decades can see how solidly entrenched we humans have become in our beliefs, defending them by any means at our disposal, even if it means killing others in the process.

The Ultimate Enlightenment For 2012

I am deeply committed to helping to change the consciousness of this planet.

I long ago accepted that this change can take place only one person at a time, and that if I am to make even the smallest contribution, it must start with me.

I invite you to find peace, to embrace peace, and ultimately, to become peace. Let this be the moment when you finally stop looking to others to do what you came here to accomplish.

This, I believe, is what Mohandas Karamchand Gandhi meant when he said, *You must be the change you wish to see in the world.*

We have all been living in illusions within the illusion, duped by the distortions and outright lies fed to us from birth by others who, for the most part, are unwitting earlier victims of the same process that befall us.

The choice before you is both immediate and unequivocal: to follow the herd or break free.

Not only do you need to awaken, but, for reasons I will explore more fully with you in the months to come, you need to awaken *now*.

The Ultimate Enlightenment For 2012

The vast majority of people around you will not wish to face these all too certain realities. They would prefer to remain anesthetized by the distractions of our affluent societies.

There is far more happening right now under our noses that you can imagine. Each new column that I file for UPI's Religion and Spirituality Forum takes me deeper into the abyss.

If you haven't been reading them, you might want to look at the latest piece about the Middle East (see previous Prism House link) as they have certainly shifted my perception of what this struggle is all about and how it was deliberately engineered as part of a far greater agenda.

Perhaps when you begin to see the larger game afoot, you will come to understand who you really are and how vitally important you are to the solution. The answer ultimately lies within each of us. *What we make of ourselves determines the fate of those we would wish to see changed.*

I do not ask for agreement on this, only that you find the courage to go more deeply within yourself that you have ever done before. *Let your heart be your guide.* There is a very bright light at the end of this exceedingly long and dark tunnel, but it will not come from the UN, the Vatican, or the White House.

The Ultimate Enlightenment For 2012

If it is to come at all, it must come from us.

Please share this message with those who are meant to be part of the solution. There have already been enough candles and vigils and prayers and meditations and emails to shift the tide of events fifty times over, and yet they continue.

Now there's some real work to be done.

Jean-Claude Koven is a writer and speaker based in Rancho Mirage, CA. He is the author of <u>Going Deeper: How To Make Sense of Your Life When Your Life Makes No Sense</u>, the Allbook's Reviews editor's choice for the best metaphysical book of 2004.

He was also the recipient of USABookNews.com best metaphysical book award. For more information, please visit http://www.prismhouse.com/

Copyright © 2005

Jean-Claude Koven – All Rights Reserved

This article is copyrighted but you have permission to share it through any medium as long as the proper copyright and credit line is included.

She Created Me

How we evolve into what we ultimately become is the question for the ages. In my case, it was neither fate nor self-determinism, but the vision of an incredible woman who conjured me into existence.

By the time I reached my early forties, I knew I was in trouble.

I had achieved almost everything I set out to accomplish in life and had little to show for it other than a respectable stock portfolio and a shoe box full of badly tarnished brass rings collected while riding society's merry-go-round.

In the world's eyes I was a successful entrepreneur; in my own I desperately wanted a do-over. I had been living someone else's life, and it was high time I showed up in my own.

Little did I know that 8,000 miles away, in Johannesburg, South Africa, Arianne, the woman who would someday become my wife, was embarking on a magical process to create the new world in which I was about to emerge.

She too wanted more, but unlike me, she had a pretty accurate idea of what it was, and what's more, she knew exactly how to make it happen.

I have asked her to repeat the story over and over again, never tiring of hearing how she created me. Each iteration reveals a little detail, a subtle nuance that somehow escaped earlier versions. I suppose every child, no matter how old, wants to know where she or he came from.

It started on a late Friday evening in April. Arianne arranged to have the house to herself for the weekend so she could devote all her energies to a ritual of creation: making a treasure map.

Just in case readers of this article would like to bake up their own new universe cake, I'll pass on the recipe.

The ingredients are easily assembled: a large sheet of drawing board or stiff paper (2 feet by 3 feet), a dozen or so picture magazines you enjoy reading, scissors and glue.

Arianne claims she had no idea of what to do before she began her process, but two things she did know with all her heart. One, she would be guided each step along the way. Two, whatever she envisioned would, without a sliver of a doubt, be manifested.

The Ultimate Enlightenment For 2012

Friday night Arianne began a fast that was to end only when she completed her work. Her next meal was in fact late Saturday afternoon. All she permitted herself during the process was water and a single apple.

There is something deliciously symbolic to me in the woman eating the apple out of her own hand.

Friday night, from six until ten, and again Saturday morning, from eight until noon, Arianne meditated. Her intent was to reach a higher vibrational state so she could see beyond the cloud bank that had enshrouded her life until then. She also asked that the way be cleared for her to let go of the past and be totally open to moving into a new life.

By noon on Saturday, Arianne knew she was ready. Her mind had been cleared of all preconceptions and was open to guidance from her higher self.

She set the blank drawing board before her on the table and opened the first of the magazines. She read none of the articles, confining her attention to the photos and headlines.

Without allowing her mind to enter into the process, she assumed a meditative state as she slowly turned the pages, waiting for something to jump out at her.

The Ultimate Enlightenment For 2012

By the time she was halfway through the fifth magazine, the message on the Treasure Map had begun revealing itself. She had already found three key elements, carefully cut them out, and placed them on the board.

The first was a beautiful color photo of one of her youthful heartthrobs, Jean-Claude Killy, the French skier who won three gold medals at the 1968 Winter Olympics in Grenoble, France.

Arianne admits to having always wanted a French lover. It wasn't until long after we'd been married that she discovered I had been a ski patrolman for many years before we met.

The second and third photos were of a beautiful home and a shiny new car. Arianne had always lived in homes that belonged to someone else, and the one new car she had ever owned, one of the original Volkswagen Beetles, was stolen a few days after she had used the last of her savings to buy it.

She spent hours going through the rest of the magazines, allowing enough time for each page to speak to her. Occasionally a photo or word glowed with radiance, a few fairly shouted out to her, but most faded into a haze, letting her know they were not to be part of her map.

The Ultimate Enlightenment For 2012

Arianne reverently cut out each element that caught her attention. By the time she was ready to glue each piece into its final resting place she had selected about a dozen symbols of her future universe.

Each piece was moved again and again until it linked perfectly with all the others and the mosaic sprang to life.

A small map of the United States was in the lower right-hand corner, just below a cutout of a jet plane that represented traveling to the four corners of the Earth.

Up near the top were the words "financial" and "security." There were five different renderings of "love," some encased in beautiful hearts.

Fairies and angels blessed her creation from their perches near the top.

When she finished the ritual, it was almost dark, but she could see her future world looming before her, and she liked what she saw.

She mounted the map on her bedroom wall so it would be the first thing she saw upon rising and the last thing before she closed her eyes for the night. We met two months later. Not only was I welcome in the universe Arianne created, I am a fully vested co-creator.

The Ultimate Enlightenment For 2012

Our lives have been as magical as she intended, and without exception everything she envisioned has come to pass.

A few years ago we came upon a ceramic Hawaiian wishing bowl while vacationing on the Big Island.

It looks Oriental with its green cracked glaze and removable bamboo-shaped lid on which is tied a leather thong that holds a suspended capsule.

Each of us has our own tightly rolled-up piece of paper inside the capsule. On it we write our next set of wishes. As each comes true, we give thanks, pull out the paper, and write down the next intended manifestation.

This is how we live our lives, taking responsibility for knowing what we want and focusing our attention to make it happen.

From time to time I think back on where my other life might have taken me, but I don't really see much. Things are much clearer when I see myself fully here in the world.

Arianne crafted for the two of us that one April weekend more than twenty years ago. The future is limited only by our imaginations and our willingness to let go of the past and enter into it.

The Ultimate Enlightenment For 2012

Now it's my turn to open new doors of exploration. I've become curious about the infinite potential in relationships and have already written the first three chapters of a new book that deals with how men must evolve in order to coexist with the emerging divine feminine energy that is leading us all into the next paradigm.

From here on in I'm breaking new ground, and I need to actually experience each of the teachings and initiations that await the main character.

I've been given a clear picture of what lies ahead, and the thrill of the adventure has me well in its clutches. Women will soon learn to evoke and embrace their Aphrodite, the archetype of divine femininity.

As they perfect the ability to embrace this exquisite energy, a beautiful tree of grace, beauty, and wisdom will begin to grow within their being.

Men will have to become so sure, so strong within themselves that they can readily surrender to that divine feminine and hold space for the magic tree to grow.

It is the man's job to shower it with adoration so pure and complete that the blossoms of the tree are pollinated and develop into the celestial fruit that will transport the lovers into the next dimension of being.

The Ultimate Enlightenment For 2012

This is the journey that awaits us all as we learn that true freedom comes from the willingness to love with such complete abandonment that one is ready to lose oneself completely in the process of merging.

To know this is to know that all is One.

Jean-Claude Koven is a writer and speaker based in Rancho Mirage, CA. He is the <u>author of Going Deeper: How To Make Sense of Your Life When Your Life Makes No Sense</u>, the Allbook's Reviews editor's choice for the best metaphysical book of 2004.

He was also the recipient of USABookNews.com best metaphysical book award. For more information, please visit http://www.goingdeeper.org

Copyright © 2005

Jean-Claude Koven – All Rights Reserved

This article is copyrighted but you have permission to share it through any medium as long as the proper copyright and credit line is included.

Epilogue

I am making my way towards a new reality. The thoughts in keeping with doing so are forever impinging upon my consciousness. I am now finding that I am more easily able to detach from the sensationalism, thereby attuning my focus on more important matters.

I am becoming more relaxed in the administrative dealings associated with my current role as a Special Education teacher. In lifting and releasing myself from the bondage of the past, sending it outwards as a ripple or domino effect, I am also serving Mother Gaia in her splendor and beauty.

Might this be what Jesus meant when he spoke of being of this world and yet not of this world?

If one but takes the time to look about them with spiritual eyes, one will find beauty and harmony in abundance. There are people who do not yet understand that an increase in one's vibratory level serves to bring about remarkable changes. The more enlightened we become, the less likely we are attracted to the darker energies that exist, gradually pulling away from their influence. In so doing, we reclaim our power.

The Ultimate Enlightenment For 2012

As humanity continues to grow in this way, these dual energies of light and dark become more separated, allowing for major changes to take place.

If I may return to words shared by Nick Bunick.

You are not a human being, that by coincidence, has a spirit and a soul. You are a spirit with a soul that is having a human experience. [178]

In keeping, we are sparks of the divine.

We are beings of light.

It is important, therefore, to think openly, to allow one's mind to expand.

We, alone, have been responsible for allowing others to impose restrictions upon us; this is what must be undone.

In the re-discovering of who humans ultimately are, this knowledge will bring great happiness and relief to millions of people.

---

[178] Bunick, Nick. (1998). *In God's Truth* (p. 75). Charlottesville, VA: Hampton Roads Publishing Company, Inc.

The Ultimate Enlightenment For 2012

Now is the time to forge ahead with utmost confidence, knowing that with each step forward you will never return to that which you have left behind, for this is the necessary and much needed action, the action that leads one to experience much in the way of liberation and freedom.

As I write these words, energies are changing. What you give your focus to can only expand. Do not worry about the how of the focus. As you are standing in a thought, or in a word, or in an action that feels good to you, "then you are fully open and allowing all of that Divine Energy to flow through you." [179]

For in this moment that "you are all that you said you would be when you decided to come forth into this body. You are an extension of pure positive energy. You are in your full creative power. You are thriving. You are clear-minded. You are joyful. You are filled with love. You are who you are – allowing that which you really are." [180]

---

[179] Abraham-Hicks Publications. (2006). *Daily Quotation*. Excerpted from a workshop in North Los Angeles, CA on Sunday, August 18th, 2002. Retrieved via email digest from http://www.abraham-hicks.com/
[180] Ibid.

We are vibrational beings. That which we focus upon becomes the way in which we set our individual tuner and "when you focus there for as little as 17 seconds, you activate that vibration within you." [181]

This is so incredibly exciting because "once you activate a vibration within you, Law of Attraction begins responding to that vibration," [182] whether something wanted or unwanted; hence, the saying, *be careful what you wish for*.

In keeping, my vibrations are rising so as to draw increased spiritual energies my way. In this way, a great cleansing is taking place within this physical body.

Likewise, conscious change must start with me.

When the majority of humanity has reached the same level of conscious desire and intent, the changes focused upon shall come into fruition, much akin with the As Above, So Below adage.

---

[181] Abraham-Hicks Publications. (2006). *Daily Quotation*. Excerpted from a workshop in Syracuse, NY on Saturday, September 30th, 2000. Retrieved via email digest from http://www.abraham-hicks.com/
[182] Ibid.

The Ultimate Enlightenment For 2012

All that is good and wholesome will manifest and, as a result, humanity will have entered into an expanded consciousness.

This process has already begun.

If you are not sure about yourself, just look back a few years and you will quickly realize how much you have changed.

What has begun can only increase in momentum.

Giving kind and loving thoughts in appreciation, without any thought of restricting this flow, seeing the beauty and perfection that underlies all that is seen and experienced, such can only raise one's vibration.

One must endeavor to see beyond the physical, especially where people are concerned; herein lies the biggest challenge that each faces, for all have the potential to change.

If I may share what I have gleaned, Dharma means the carrier of goodness and wholesomeness and Hu means light, as in you are the light of God.

When you spread darkness, you go opposite your dharma. When you slander someone, you go opposite your dharma.

The Ultimate Enlightenment For 2012

One only has to raise one's consciousness in order to begin to see how it is indeed possible to leave behind the old patterning and accepted ways of behavior, thereby enabling one to embrace those that are more in alignment with one's real self.

For myself, I resonate with many stones of the mineral kingdom; some of which are Amber (fossilized plant resin, taking millions of years to create), Anorthosite (about 1.2 billion years old and also found on the moon), Apophylite, Azeztulite, Covelite, Herkimer Diamonds (which are between 400 and 500 million years old), Jet (a form of fossilized lignite coal), Kunzite, Lapis Lazuli, Larimar, Lemurian Seed Crystals, Lepidolite, Libyan Desert Glass or LDG (about 30 million years old), Lithium Quartz (also known as Li-Quartz), Messina Ajoite, Moldavite (about 15 million years old), Nuummite (about 3 billion years old), Phenacite, Quantum Quattro Silica or QQS (made up of 5 minerals: Shattuckite, Chrysocolla, Dioptase, Malachite and Smoky Quartz), Septarian (a composite of fossilized sea creatures that turned into Calcite and Aragonite, thereby creating marvelous colors and patterns), Seraphinite, Spider Jasper, Sugilite, Tibetan DT crystals and Variscite.

The energies of these stones are serving to bring my vibrations in line with that which is reflective of the very metaphysical properties attributed to these gems of the

Earth, all of which reflect back to me as increased feelings of peace and contentment.

The person I am today has no bearing on the person that I was several years ago.

As one's energy encompasses a larger area, all who come within that individual's aura cannot help but be positively reflected.

In keeping, as this power grows exponentially upon this planet, it serves to uplift others, with results noted as remarkable increases in the mass consciousness of man.

The Law of Attraction merely amplifies the vibration that exists within. Every person on the planet is affected by it.

The Law of Attraction means that "it is always true that what I think and what I feel and what I get are always a match, and there is not a person on the planet that did not know that when they were born, and there is not a person on the planet that would not benefit by knowing it. But many, many, many are not yet asking and therefore are not yet ready for the answer. And so, we would say that, although

The Ultimate Enlightenment For 2012

everyone wants the information, everyone is not necessarily ready for it." [183]

With over 6.5 billion people sharing this planet, this means that there are 6.5 billion realities, viewpoints, truths, opinions and ways of expressing; you simply have to recognize that which is yours, for you, alone, must walk your path.

---

[183] Abraham-Hicks Publications. (2006). *Daily Quotation*. Excerpted from a workshop in San Diego, CA on Saturday, February 7th, 1988. Retrieved via email digest from http://www.abraham-hicks.com/

Bibliography

Ambrose, Kala. (2007) *9 Life Altering Lessons: Secrets of the Mystery Schools Unveiled.*

Austin, June. (2006) *Genesis of Man.*

Braden, Gregg. (1995) *Awakening to Zero Point: The Collective Initiation.*

Braden, Gregg. (1997) *Walking Between the Worlds: The Science of Compassion.*

Braden, Gregg. (2000) *The Isaiah Effect: Decoding the Lost Science of Prayer and Prophecy.*

Braden, Gregg. (2000) *Beyond Zero Point: The Journey to Compassion.*

Braden, Gregg. (2004) *The God Code: The Secret of Our Past, The Promise of Our Future.*

Braden, Gregg. (2004) *The Divine Name: Sounds of the God Code.* (Audio Book)

Braden, Gregg. (2005) *The Lost Mode of Prayer.* (Audio CD)

Braden, Gregg. (2005) *Unleashing The Power of The God Code: The Mystery and Meaning of the Message in Our Cells.* (Audio CD)

Braden, Gregg. (2005) *An Ancient Magical Prayer: Insights from the Dead Sea Scrolls.* (Audio Book)

Braden, Gregg. (2005) *Speaking the Lost Language of God: Awakening the Forgotten Wisdom of Prayer, Prophecy and the Dead Sea Scrolls.* (Audio Book)

Braden, Gregg. (2005) *Awakening the Power of A Modern God: Unlock the Mystery and Healing of Your Spiritual DNA.* (Audio Book)

Braden, Gregg. (2006) *Secrets of The Lost Mode of Prayer.*

Braden, Gregg. (2007) *The Divine Matrix: Bridging Time, Space, Miracles and Belief.*

Breathnach, Sarah Ban. (1996) *Simple Abundance: A Daybook of Comfort and Joy.*

Breathnach, Sarah Ban. (2000) *The Simple Abundance Companion: Following Your Authentic Path To Something More.*

Bunick, Nick. (1998) In *God's Truth.*

Chopra, Deepak. (1998) *The Path to Love: Spiritual Strategies for Healing*.

Chopra, Deepak. (2005) *Peace Is The Way: Bringing War and Violence to An End*.

Coelho, Paulo. (1998) *The Alchemist*.

Coelho, Paulo. (2003) *Warrior Of The Light*.

Das, Lama Surys. (1998) *Awakening the Buddha Within*.

Das, Lama Surys. (2000) *Awakening to the Sacred: Creating a Spiritual Life From Scratch*.

Das, Lama Surys. (2001) *Awakening the Buddhist Heart: Integrating Love, Meaning and Connection into Every Part of Your Life*.

Das, Lama Surys. (2003) *Living Kindness: The Buddha's Ten Guiding Principles for a Blessed Life*.

Das, Lama Surys. (2003) *Letting Go of the Person You Used To Be: Lessons on Change, Loss and Spiritual Transformation*.

Doucette, Michele. (2007) *Turn Off The TV and Turn On Your Mind*. (ebook)

Doucette, Michele. (2010) *A Travel in Time to Grand Pré*. (second edition)

Dyer, Wayne. (1998) *Manifest Your Destiny: The Nine Spiritual Principles For Getting Everything That You Want*.

Dyer, Wayne. (2002) *Getting in the Gap: Making Conscious Contact with God Through Meditation*. (Book and CD)

Gawain, Shakti. (1993) *Living In The Light: A Guide to Personal and Planetary Transformation*.

Gawain, Shakti. (1999) *The Four Levels of Healing*.

Gawain, Shakti. (2000) *The Path of Transformation: How Healing Ourselves Can Change The World*.

Gawain, Shakti. (2003) *Reflections in The Light: Daily Thoughts and Affirmations*.

Gelb, Michael. (2005) *Da Vinci Decoded*.

Hansard, Christopher. (2003) *The Tibetan Art of Positive Thinking*.

Hicks, Esther and Hicks, Jerry. (2004) *Ask and It Is Given: Learning to Manifest Your Desires*.

Hicks, Esther and Hicks, Jerry. (2004) *The Teachings of Abraham: Well-Being Cards.*

Hicks, Esther and Hicks, Jerry. (2005) *The Amazing Power of Deliberate Intent: Living the Art of Allowing.*

Hicks, Esther and Hicks, Jerry. (2006) *The Law of Attraction: The Basics of the Teachings of Abraham.*

Hicks, Esther and Hicks, Jerry. (2008) *The Astonishing Power of Emotions: Let Your Feelings Be Your Guide.*

Hicks, Esther and Hicks, Jerry. (2009) *The Vortex: Where The Law of Attraction Assembles all Cooperative Relationships.*

Ingram, Julia. (2004) *The Lost Sisterhood: The Return of Mary Magdalene, the Mother Mary, and Other Holy Women.*

Johnson, Bettye. (2005) *Secrets of the Magdalene Scrolls: The Forbidden Truth of the Life and Times of Mary Magdalene.*

Johnson, Bettye. (2007) *Mary Magdalene, Her Legacy.*

Johnson, Bettye. (2008) *Awakening the Genie Within.*

Koven, Jean-Claude. (2004) *Going Deeper: How To Make Sense of Your Life When Your Life Makes No Sense*.

Lama, Dalai. (2004) *The Wisdom of Forgiveness: Intimate Conversations and Journey*.

Lyons, Lona. (2007) *The Magdalene Dispensation*.

Lyons, Lona. (2008) *Daughter of Magdalene*.

McTaggart, Lynne. (2003) *The Field: The Quest For The Secret Force Of The Universe*.

McTaggart, Lynne. (2008) *The Intention Experiment: Using Your Thoughts to Change Your Life and the World*.

Millman, Dan. (2000) *Way of the Peaceful Warrior*.

Millman, Dan. (1991) *Sacred Journey of the Peaceful Warrior*.

Millman, Dan. (1992) *No ordinary Moments: A Peaceful Warrior's Guide to Daily Life*.

Millman, Dan. (1995) *The Life You Were Born To Live*.

Millman, Dan. (1999) *Everyday Enlightenment*.

Morgan, Marlo. (1995) *Mutant Message Down Under*.

Morgan, Marlo. (1998) *Mutant Messages From Forever: A Novel of Aboriginal Wisdom.*

Nichols, L. Joseph. (2000) *The Soul As Healer: Lessons in Affirmation, Visualization and Inner Power.*

Peniel, Jon. (1998) *The Lost Teachings of Atlantis: The Children of The Law of One.*

Peniel, Jon. (1999) *The Golden Rule Workbook: A Manual for the New Millennium.*

Price, John Randolph. (1987) *The Superbeings.*

Price, John Randolph. (1998) *The Success Book.*

Quinn, Gary. (2003) *Experience Your Greatness: Give Yourself Permission To Live.* (Audio CD)

Redfield, James. (1995) *The Celestine Prophecy.*

Redfield, James. (1997) *The Celestine Vision: Living the New Spiritual Awareness.*

Redfield, James. (1998) *The Tenth Insight.*

Redfield, James. (1999) *The Secret of Shambhala.*

Renard, Gary. (2004) *The Disappearance of the Universe.*

Renard, Gary. (2006) *Your Immortal Reality: How To Break the Cycle of Birth and Death.*

Ruiz, Don Miguel. (1997) *The Four Agreements: A Practical Guide to Personal Freedom.*

Ruiz, Don Miguel. (1999) *The Mastery of Love: A Practical Guide to The Art of Relationship.*

Ruiz, Don Miguel. (2000) *The Four Agreements Companion Book.*

Ruiz, Don Miguel. (2004) *The Voice of Knowledge: A Practical Guide to Inner Peace.*

Ruiz, Don Miguel. (2009) *Fifth Agreement: A Practical Guide to Self-Mastery.*

Schuman, Helen. (1997) *A Course in Miracles.*

Schwartz, Robert. (2009) *Your Soul's Plan: Discovering the Real Meaning of the Life You Planned Before You Were Born.*

Sharma, Robin. (1997) *The Monk Who Sold His Ferrari.*

Sharma, Robin. (2005) *Big Ideas to Live Your Best Life: Discover Your Destiny.*

Shinn, Florence Scovel. (1989) The *Wisdom of Florence Scovel Shinn.*

Shinn, Florence Scovel. (1991) *The Game of Life Affirmation and Inspiration Cards: Positive Words For A Positive Life.*

Shinn, Florence Scovel. (2006) *The Game of Life.* (Book and CD)

Tolle, Eckhart. (1999) *The Power of Now: A Guide to Spiritual Enlightenment.*

Tolle, Eckhart. (2001) *Practicing the Power of Now: Meditations, Exercises and Core Teachings for Living the Liberated Life.*

Tolle, Eckhart. (2001) *The Realization of Being: A Guide to Experiencing Your True Identity.* (Audio CD)

Tolle, Eckhart. (2003) *Stillness Speaks.*

Tolle, Eckhart. (2003) *Entering The Now.* (Audio CD)

Tolle, Eckhart. (2005) *A New Earth: Awakening to Your Life's Purpose.*

Twyman, James. (1998) *Emissary of Peace: A Vision of Light.*

Twyman, James. (2000) *The Secret of the Beloved Disciple.*

Twyman, James. (2000) *Portrait of the Master*.

Twyman, James. (2000) *Praying Peace: In Conversation with Gregg Braden and Doreen Virtue*.

Twyman, James. (2003) *The Proposing Tree*.

Twyman, James. (2008) *The Moses Code: The Most Powerful Manifestation Tool in the History of the World*.

Twyman, James. (2009) *The Kabbalah Code: A True Adventure*.

Twyman, James. (2009) *The Proof: A 40-Day Program for Embodying Oneness*.

Vanzant, Iyanla. (2000) *Until Today*.

Virtue, Doreen. (1997) *The Lightworker's Way*.

Virtue, Doreen. (2006) *Divine Magic: The Seven Sacred Secrets of Manifestation*. (Book and CD)

Walker, Ethan III. (2003) *The Mystic Christ: The Light of Non-Duality and the Path of Love According to the Life and Teachings of Jesus*.

Walsch, Neale Donald. (1999) *Abundance and Right Livelihood: Applications for Living*.

Walsch, Neale Donald. (2000) *Bringers of The Light*.

Walsch, Neale Donald. (2002) *The New Revelations: A Conversation with God*.

Walters, J. Donald. (2000) *Awaken to Superconsciousness: How To Use Meditation for Inner Peace, Intuitive Guidance and Greater Awareness*.

Walters, J. Donald. (2000) *Meditations to Awaken Superconsciousness: Guided Meditations on The Light* (audio cassette).

Walters, J. Donald. (2003) *Meditation for Starters*. (Book and CD)

Walters, J. Donald. (2003) *Metaphysical Meditations*. (Audio CD)

Walters, J. Donald. (2003) *Secrets of Bringing Peace On Earth*.

Weiss, Brian. (2001) *Messages From the Masters: Tapping Into The Power of Love*.

Weiss, Brian. (2002) *Meditation: Achieving Inner Peace and Tranquility in Your Life*.

Williamson, Marianne. (1996) *A Return To Love*.

Williamson, Marianne. (1997) *Morning and Evening Meditations and Prayers*.

Williamson, Marianne. (2002) *Everyday Grace: Having Hope, Finding Forgiveness and Making Miracles*.

Williamson, Marianne. (2003) *Being In Light*. (Audio CD set)

Yogananda, Paramahansa. (1979) *Metaphysical Meditations: Universal Prayers, Affirmations and Visualizations*.

Yogananda, Paramahansa. (2004) *The Second Coming of Christ: The Resurrection of the Christ Within You*.

Zukav, Gary. (1998) *The Seat of The Soul*.

Zukav, Gary. (2001) *Thoughts from The Seat of The Soul: Meditations for Souls in Process*.

Zukav, Gary and Francis, Linda. (2001) *The Heart of The Soul: Emotional Awareness*.

Zukav, Gary and Francis, Linda. (2003) *The Mind of The Soul: Responsible Choice*.

Zukav, Gary and Francis, Linda. (2003) *Self-Empowerment Journal: A Companion to The Mind of The Soul: Responsible Choice.*

Zukav, Gary. (2010) *Spiritual Partnership: The Journey to Authentic Power.*

About the Author

Michele Doucette is webmistress of Portals of Spirit, a spirituality site whereby one will find links to (1) an ezine called Gateway To The Soul, (2) books of spiritual resonance, (3) categories of interest from Angels to Zen, (4) Soulutions, (5) up-to-date information as shared by a Quantum Healer, (6) healing resource advertisements and (7) spiritual news.

In addition, she holds a Crystal Healing Practitioner diploma (Stonebridge College in the UK). As a Level 2 Reiki Practitioner, she sends long distance Reiki to those who make the request, claiming only to be a channeler of the Universal Energy, thereby allowing the individual(s) in question to heal themselves.

www.ingramcontent.com/pod-product-compliance
Lightning Source LLC
Chambersburg PA
CBHW061944070426
42450CB00007BA/1045